GOOD/BAD
DAD/DAD

Do's and Don'ts from the Trenches

GOOD/BAD DAD/DAD

Do's and Don'ts from the Trenches

David George

ALPHA

A member of Penguin Group (USA) Inc.

ALPHA BOOKS

Published by the Penguin Group

Penguin Group (USA) Inc., 375 Hudson Street, New York, New York 10014, U.S.A.

Penguin Group (Canada), 10 Alcorn Avenue, Toronto, Ontario, Canada M4V 3B2 (a division of Pearson Penguin Canada Inc.)

Penguin Books Ltd, 80 Strand, London WC2R 0RL, England

Penguin Ireland, 25 St Stephen's Green, Dublin 2, Ireland (a division of Penguin Books Ltd)

Penguin Group (Australia), 250 Camberwell Road, Camberwell, Victoria 3124, Australia (a division of Pearson Australia Group Pty Ltd)

Penguin Books India Pvt Ltd, 11 Community Centre, Panchsheel Park, New Delhi—110 017, India

Penguin Group (NZ), cnr Airborne and Rosedale Roads, Albany, Auckland 1310, New Zealand (a division of Pearson New Zealand Ltd)

Penguin Books (South Africa) (Pty) Ltd, 24 Sturdee Avenue, Rosebank, Johannesburg 2196, South Africa

Penguin Books Ltd, Registered Offices: 80 Strand, London WC2R 0RL, England

International Standard Book Number: 978-1-59257-604-3
Library of Congress Catalog Card Number: 2006934450

09 08 07   8 7 6 5 4 3 2 1

Interpretation of the printing code: The rightmost number of the first series of numbers is the year of the book's printing; the rightmost number of the second series of numbers is the number of the book's printing. For example, a printing code of 07-1 shows that the first printing occurred in 2007.

Printed in the United States of America

Note: This publication contains the opinions and ideas of its author. It is intended to provide helpful and informative material on the subject matter covered. It is sold with the understanding that the author and publisher are not engaged in rendering professional services in the book. If the reader requires personal assistance or advice, a competent professional should be consulted.

The author and publisher specifically disclaim any responsibility for any liability, loss, or risk, personal or otherwise, which is incurred as a consequence, directly or indirectly, of the use and application of any of the contents of this book.

Trademarks: All terms mentioned in this book that are known to be or are suspected of being trademarks or service marks have been appropriately capitalized. Alpha Books and Penguin Group (USA) Inc. cannot attest to the accuracy of this information. Use of a term in this book should not be regarded as affecting the validity of any trademark or service mark.

Most Alpha books are available at special quantity discounts for bulk purchases for sales promotions, premiums, fundraising, or educational use. Special books, or book excerpts, can also be created to fit specific needs.

For details, write: Special Markets, Alpha Books, 375 Hudson Street, New York, NY 10014.

To Zachary and Alex, for making me the best Good Dad I could be.

To Maureen, for making me the best husband and father I could be.

To Wanda, my mother, for making me.

CONTENTS

DO

READ THIS INTRODUCTION IF YOU WANT TO BE THE BEST GOOD DAD YOU CAN BE.

I'm beginning this book with a question and I'd like you to answer it to the best of your ability. Ready? Here goes:

Do you consider yourself a Good Dad or a Bad Dad?

Okay, pencils down. Without fail, every single person in possession of the Y chromosome answers, "*Good Dad.*" And why not? Who would ever think of themselves otherwise?

But chances are … you're a little of both.

Now before you round up all the other dads in the village and come looking for me with torches blazing, hear me out, because it's not as bad as it sounds.

Everybody wants to be a Good Dad. It's in our DNA. We're hard-wired to propagate, to protect, to nurture, to teach, to guide, and, ultimately, to release our progeny into the world so they, too, can pass along their genes to their children, and their children's children. It's all done to carry on the species. It's bigger than us, it's a primordial juggernaut, and we can't stop it.

Yes, we're dads, but, first and foremost, we're human. Meaning we're not perfect. We make mistakes in everything we do, no matter how hard we try. Look at it this way—we're good drivers, but occasionally we get a ticket. We're good employees, but at times we duck out early. We're good husbands, but once in a while we're not as attentive as we could be.

You see where this is going, don't you? There's good and bad in all of us, even when it comes to fatherhood. No matter how good of a dad you are, you will, on occasion, sprout hair, grow fangs, howl at the moon, and turn into—gasp!—*the Bad Dad*. And chances are you won't even know it. For example, I know this one dad, a real good guy, who puts a box of cereal in his kids' bedroom on weekend nights. Why? So when they wake up they can eat breakfast while he catches an extra half-hour of sleep!

Bad Dad.

Like I said, most Good Dads who fall prey to the dark side don't even realize they're lapsing into Bad Dad behavior. Like the preceding cereal incident, most Bad Dad moments are nothing more than a momentary lapse in judgment. An honest mistake. A small human blunder. However, the consequences of some Bad Dad moments can be a little more critical. Like not baby-proofing your house. Or finally getting around to starting a college fund … when your child is 17.

So what's the best way to avoid Bad Dad behavior? To be as informed as you can be. And that's why I wrote *Good Dad/Bad Dad: Do's and Don'ts from the Trenches.*

You see, my father died at age 45 of a heart attack. I was 3 months old. From that point on I grew up in a household entirely of women. A mom and four older sisters. Consequently, I had no male role model in my life. More to the point, no *Dad* role model. No one to show me the ropes such as how to bait a hook, tie a square-knot, throw a curveball, or pitch a tent. I never had a dad to help me through my teen years. Or my college years. Or young adulthood. No beacon of knowledge to steer toward when I desperately needed advice.

Fast-forward to now. I'm married to a wonderful woman and am blessed with two beautiful children. Both boys. (How's that for irony?) After the birth of my first son, it hit me: I have absolutely no idea what I'm doing. No clue how to raise a child. I was the youngest in my family, the only boy, with no dad, and all of a sudden I'm supposed to be fluent in fatherhood? I don't think so.

I must admit those first years were rough. I made a lot of Bad Dad mistakes. Nothing too detrimental to the kids', I hope, but I wish someone would have been there to grab me by the lapels and bark, "You idiot—don't do that, do this." I had to figure out a lot of stuff myself. When I did make the right decision, when I really was the Good Dad, I felt triumphant and empowered.

Good Dad/Bad Dad: Do's and Don'ts from the Trenches will make you feel triumphant and empowered, too, with useful tips, advice, guidance, counsel, teachings, instructions, lessons, input, advice, and encouragement for being the best Good Dad you can be. I even throw in a few recipes for you to try, not to mention a smattering of fascinating facts and figures on what it means to be a dad.

Some things in the book I experienced firsthand or learned from other dads. Other topics I researched in magazines, books, newspapers, or on the Internet. I took great care in how I presented the material, too. For one thing, I didn't get too preachy. I don't like being lectured to, and I'm pretty sure you don't either. My goal was to make *Good Dad/Bad Dad: Do's and Don'ts from the Trenches* sound like you're getting expert advice from your favorite drinking buddy—minus the slurring—because I want it to be fun and engaging while still managing to be highly informative.

Also, because most guys have the attention span of a gnat, I kept the chapters as short as I could. That way you get the core message without having to wade through reams of encyclopedia-like verbiage. Hey, *Good Dad/Bad Dad: Do's and Don'ts from the Trenches* tells it like it really is—sans the fluff—with a touch of humor, a modicum of sarcasm, and a whole lot of heart.

One last point: most of the information presented is meant to instruct, but admittedly there are a few items that are more—how shall I put it?—controversial. So when you find yourself disagreeing with me on a certain point, and believe me you will, don't dismiss the information right away. Think about it, compare it with what you believe, and *then* reject it or accept it. The two contrasting viewpoints, when put side-by-side, might help you think of an even better course of action, making you an even better dad. You know the expression "20/20 hindsight"? That's what this book has. But to you, the reader, it's 20/20 *insight*.

In the end, we must remember that it's not about us, it's about our kids. Be the best dad you can be, and your kids will be the best they can be.

Now get reading.

DON'T
SKIP THIS ACKNOWLEDGEMENTS PAGE, YOU'LL ENJOY IT.

If there was an award show that had a category for *Best Non-Fiction Book on Parenting with Good Dad/Bad Dad in the Title*—and I won—here are the people I would thank in my acceptance speech.

"Oh, wow, this is unbelievable. I'm so nervous. Whew, first of all, I'd like to thank my Editorial Director Mike Sanders of Alpha Books for believing in me and the book. I couldn't have done it without his help and support. I'd also like to thank my publisher, Marie Butler-Knight, for green lighting the book, and Phil Kitchel, Janette Lynn, and Tricia Liebig for their insights and contributions. Then there's…

(ORCHESTRAL MUSIC UP)

"Hey, I'm not finished yet! There's also James Hunter Ross, Gary Sanchez, Carmen Dorr, Scot Boland, Cindy deJong…

(FADING INTO THE DISTANCE)

…*my sisters Mary Jane, Patty, Kathy and Debbie…I hope I'm not forgetting anybody….*

1

**BABY-PROOF
YOUR HOUSE**

Funny thing. I baby-proofed my house, but they got in anyway. (Rim shot) "Thank you, I'll be here all week."

Actually, it's no joking matter. Definitely, positively, without a doubt, baby-proof your house. Hidden dangers lurk everywhere. From crib mattresses that can suffocate to pull-cords that can strangle.

Babies are naturally curious. That's how they learn. They love to explore, investigate, analyze, delve, examine, scrutinize, and inspect anything they can see, hear, smell, taste, or touch. Put yourself in their booties. You've been in a dark, insulated environment for 9 months, when all of a sudden you're thrust into a foreign land surrounded by light and color and noise and shapes. After you're mobile, what are you going to do? Get your hands on everything you can. And I mean everything. Ordinary, everyday objects we take for granted are eureka moments for babies.

So where do you start? The National Safety Council's website: www.nsc.org. It's got a very detailed section on the things you need to do to properly and thoroughly baby-proof your house. However, in anticipation of you being highly entertained with this book and not wanting to get up to turn on your computer, I reprinted their baby-proofing section right here in *Good Dad/Bad Dad: The Do's and Don'ts from the Trenches.* So here you go. And you're welcome.

SUFFOCATION AND CHOKING

Mechanical suffocation and suffocation by ingested objects cause the most home fatalities to children 0 to 4 years of age.

- Infants, when placed on an adult bed of any kind, can roll into the space between the wall and the mattress and suffocate. Exercise caution if sleeping in the same bed with an infant. It's possible for an infant to become wedged between your body and the mattress and suffocate. Infants should never be placed on top of soft surfaces such as sofas, large soft toys, sofa cushions, pillows, or waterbeds or on top of blankets, quilts, or comforters.

- Babies should sleep on their backs.

- Crib bars should be no more than $2\frac{3}{8}$ inches apart to prevent infants from getting their heads stuck between them. Cribs manufactured after 1974 must meet this and other strict safety standards.

- The crib mattress must fit tightly so there are no gaps for an infant to fall into. Keep the crib clear of plastic sheets, pillows, and large stuffed animals or toys. These can be suffocation hazards.

- Keep toys with long strings or cords away from infants and young children. A cord can become wrapped around an infant's neck and cause strangulation. Toys with long strings, cords, loops, or ribbons should never be hung in cribs or playpens. Similarly, pacifiers should never be attached to strings or ribbons around the baby's neck.

- Place an infant or child's bed away from windows. Check window coverings for potentially hazardous pull-cords.

- Use child safety gates at the top and bottom of all staircases and be sure they're installed correctly. Avoid accordion-style safety gates with large openings that children could fit their heads through.

- Choking is a common cause of unintentional death in children under the age of 1. Avoid all foods that could lodge in a child's throat. Some examples include popcorn, grapes, foods with pits, raisins, nuts, hard candies, raw vegetables, and small pieces of hotdogs.

- Never let children of any age eat or suck on anything, such as hard candy, while lying down.

- Keep floors, tables, and cabinet tops free of small objects that could be swallowed. Such objects include coins, button-sized batteries, rings, nails, tacks, and broken or deflated balloons.

FALLS AND BURNS

- A mixer faucet on the basin, tub, and shower will prevent scalds. Set your hot water thermostat at 120°F. A baby's bathwater should be 100°F. Always check bathwater temperature with your wrist or elbow before putting a baby in to bathe. Don't allow children in a whirlpool, Jacuzzi, or hot tub. Their bodies are more sensitive to hot water.

- Teach youngsters that matches are tools for adults, not toys. Adults should never ignite lighters or matches in front of children. Store matches in a fire-resistant container out of the reach of youngsters.

- Do not smoke, use matches, or drink hot beverages while holding an infant. Don't leave burning cigarettes unattended.

- Remember that radiators, heating vents, space heaters, fireplaces, stoves, and hot water taps are not always hot. Children can touch them once safely and receive a severe burn the next time.

- Keep electrical cords and wires out of the way so toddlers can't pull, trip, or chew on them. Cover wall outlets with safety caps.

DROWNING

- Never leave a child unsupervised in the bathtub. If you must leave the room for a telephone call or to answer the door, wrap the child in a towel and take him or her with you. Don't leave a small child alone with any container of liquid, including wading pools, scrub buckets, and toilets.

- A swimming pool drowning could also be called a "silent death" as there is rarely a splash or cry for help to alert parents to the problem. The typical drowning victim is a boy between 1 and 3 years old who is thought not to be in the pool area at the time of the incident.

- Fence-in your pool completely. Doors leading to the pool area should be self-closing and self-latching or equipped with exit alarms and should never be propped open.

- Never take your eyes off children when they are in or near any body of water, not even for a second. Don't rely on inflatable devices, such as inner tubes, water wings, inflatable mattresses, and toys or other similar objects to keep a youngster afloat. Keep toys, tricycles, and other playthings away from the pool area. A toddler near the water could unexpectedly fall in.

- All pool owners and their families are encouraged to seek training in swimming, lifesaving, first aid, and cardiopulmonary resuscitation.

In addition to all this useful information, please exercise extreme caution when it comes to furniture and household fixtures as well. The Consumer Product Safety Commission reports that 8,000 to 10,000 people are injured every year as the result of shelves, bookcases, TV stands, and other types of furniture tipping over. And guess who's most at risk for injury and even death? That's right, young children. No-tip furniture brackets work well to prevent this type of accident.

Speaking of furniture, corner and edge cushions are a good idea, too. Our oldest, when he was 2, fell head-first on the sharp corner of his grandparent's end table. This led to a trip to the emergency room and five ghastly Frankenstein-like stitches. Which raises a good point: when you're at someone else's house, be extra vigilant, because odds are their house is not baby-proofed.

Oh, yeah—you know those little white caps they put on the end of spring-type doorstops to protect the door from dents? Remove them. They're a major choking hazard. And, of course, install childproof locks or latches on all cabinets reachable by little hands.

Baby-proofing your house does take some time, if you want to do it right. My suggestion is to do it before the baby arrives. When you're walking around like some daddy zombie due to night after night of sleep deprivation, you'll be glad you did. However, if you do wait 'til after the baby arrives, definitely do it before your little one becomes mobile.

Got money? There are companies who will come into your home and do the whole thing for you from top to bottom. It ain't cheap, but if you can swing the dough, why not? Saves you a lot of time and energy: two things you'll desperately need when your little bundle of joy arrives on the scene.

So baby-proof your house. Now. Yes, they'll still get in. But at least they'll be safe.

"Done."

"Don't worry, dear, I'll get around to it. What's that you say? Whose water just broke?"

GOOD DAD

BAD DAD

2

START A COLLEGE FUND FOR EACH CHILD AS SOON AS POSSIBLE

I'm not saying to call your financial advisor while your wife is in the delivery room, but I am suggesting you do so while your bundle of joy is still in diapers. Why? Because the one advantage you have when funding your children's education is time. Time, in this case, literally is money.

But first things first. Why a college fund? Because college takes a whole lot of funds, that's why.. After doing some digging on the Internet, I found that the cost of sending your child to a 4-year college, with on-campus living arrangements, is anywhere from $40,000 to $65,000. And that's just for a state school. If you go the private school route, 4 years can set you back—are you sitting for this?—a wallet-walloping $170,000. And that's at today's prices. Imagine what it's going to be 18 years from now.

Okay, you can now pick yourself up off the floor because, like I said earlier, you have one huge advantage on your side. Time. Time is the greatest contributing factor to a well-funded fund. That's why the earlier you start, the better off you are.

There are myriad ways to pay for an education. The usual suspects are low-interest student loans, financial aid, scholarships (yeah, right), and such. But perhaps a smarter way to go is with a state-sponsored 529 Plan or a Coverdell ESA (formerly known as an Education IRA) because of the tax savings. With a 529 Plan, for example, your investment will grow tax-free for as long as your money stays in the account. And when you withdraw the money to pay for college, the distribution is tax-free as well. Same with a Coverdell ESA, but the rules are slightly different. With a little research you'll be able to find the perfect plan that works best for you.

Speaking of research, walk into any Barnes & Noble or Borders bookstores and you'll find book after book about how to save for college. If you're reeling from the reality of all this and you're too dizzy to drive, simply go online. A few worthwhile sites to visit are savingforcollege.com, collegeboard.com, fool.com (The Motley Fool website—informative and less dry than some of the others), and finance. yahoo.com.

Is your head still swimming from the costs involved in a college education? Keep this in mind, Scrooge. According to people who do this number-crunching stuff for a living, on average, people with a Bachelor's degree earn more than 62 percent than those with a high school diploma. Over a lifetime, the chasm in earning potential between a high school diploma and a B.A. (or higher) is more than $1,000,000. That's right: *one million dollars*. Is it worth it? You tell me.

Higher education is aptly named because that's exactly where the costs keep going: higher. But you'll be in good shape if you do your due diligence, contribute regularly, and give yourself plenty of time.

On second thought, maybe you *should* call your financial advisor from the delivery room.

"Forget the Porsche, what I want is for my children to go to college."

GOOD DAD

"What do you mean you didn't save your allowance?"

BAD DAD

3

DON'T
NEGLECT
YOUR HEALTH

When you decided to have kids, you swore you'd always be there for them, right? Every Good Dad does. You want to be there to answer their questions about life, you want to be there to help them in sports, you want to be there guiding them into adulthood. Allow me to let you in on a little secret, if I may: it's kind of hard to be there for your children IF YOU'RE DEAD.

Guys are notorious for ignoring their health. Or more precisely, health concerns. For some misguided reason, guys think it's macho to *not* go to a doctor. Makes us feel manly, strong. I can see it right now, some guy's talking to his buddy, grabbing his belt and hitching his pants up like a tough guy, giving a defiant sniff and clearing his throat … "Me? Nah, haven't seen a doctor in years. Healthy as a horse. Hmm? No, that mole's been there for years … I think."

Guess what, tough guy: you ain't that tough. Seeing a doctor isn't wimpy, it's smart. Whatever you've been doing to your body all these years is going to catch up to you, believe me. Do you smoke? Do you like the sun? Do you eat a lot of fast food? Do you drink too much? Do you exercise too little? Then the day will come, my friend, when you notice an ache here, a lump there, a come-out-of-nowhere mole, or a hit-you-like-a-sledgehammer pain in your chest, and you're going to be standing there with a stunned look on your face murmuring a quiet "Uh-oh."

The good news is, it doesn't have to be this way. If you want to be there for your kids—and I mean really *be* there for them—take good care of yourself. First thing, see a doctor and get a complete physical. You're going to be pricked and probed and prodded in areas even your wife never gained access to, but it's worth it. (Pray that your doctor doesn't have chubby fingers.) It's important to go through this routine once a year. That way, if some rogue cells stage a mutiny that your immune system can't fight off, you have a good chance of stopping the insurrection before it's too late. Same with atherosclerosis and other such diseases. I schedule my physicals right around my birthday; that way I don't forget.

What's next on the list? Diet and exercise.* Join a gym. Work out. Lift weights. Climb stairs. Run. Bike. Kayak. Do something physical. You know the old saying, "move it or lose it"? It's true. And when it comes to diet, a few simple changes can make a world of difference. You know the drill by now: eat more fruits and vegetables; eat fewer fatty, salty, and processed foods. It's not rocket science.

(*Before you start a workout program or change your eating habits, always talk to your doctor first and get his advice.)

And here's a Lucky Strike extra, lover boy; eating a healthy diet and getting regular exercise is like taking Viagra without having to take Viagra. That's right, men who work out and eat right have a substantially lower risk of erectile dysfunction. A recent study found that men who exercise 3 to 5 hours a week have 30 percent less risk of having erectile dysfunction.

And for all you guys who love double bacon cheeseburgers with a big side of fries, you might want to rethink your order. According to a new report, testosterone levels can drop by as much as 50 percent after eating a high-fat meal. 50 percent! Low testosterone: low libido.

So get off the couch and get to a doctor. Because when you've got your health, you've got everything. And your kids have you.

"I'm going to the gym, be back soon."

"Honey, where'd you put the cheese puffs?"

GOOD DAD

BAD DAD

4

LEARN INFANT CPR

God forbid you ever have to use it. But you know what's worse? Needing to use it and not knowing how.

Infants and small children are like danger magnets. If it's hazardous, they're attracted to it. Bodies of water, choking hazards, sharp objects, you name it—bam!—off they go to find it. As the Good Dad, you do all the things a good parent does. You baby-proof your house, you buy age-appropriate toys, you watch your kids like a hawk, but all it takes is a split second for a child to get into trouble. Serious trouble. A happy occasion such as a poolside birthday party can turn tragic in an instant. If it does, be prepared to save a life by learning infant CPR.

CPR, if you don't know already, stands for *cardio-pulmonary resuscitation*. It's used when someone, in this case an infant, goes into respiratory or cardiac arrest. Severe asthma, accidental drowning, and airway problems can all lead to a CPR situation in infants.

The following is a step-by-step guide on how to perform infant CPR, courtesy of www.iParenting.com. These instructions are for general information purposes only and are not a substitute for taking an accredited infant CPR class (more on these types of classes later).

As you go through these steps you'll notice that the ABCs (airway, breathing, circulation) of adult CPR still apply, but infants have a smaller lung capacity and a faster breathing rate than adults. Their ribcages are more fragile and their necks are shorter. All these important factors are why procedures for infant CPR differ from adult and even child CPR.

1. Assess responsiveness by gently shaking the infant's shoulder. Shout for help. When help comes, instruct them to call 911.

2. Place the infant on a hard surface such as a kitchen floor. Be extremely careful not to twist or move the neck, as there may be a spinal injury.

3. Use the Look, Listen, and Feel approach to assess the situation. *Look* for chest rises, *Listen* for breathing, *Feel* for the infant's breath on your cheek. This should take 3 to 5 seconds. If the infant is struggling to breathe, do not perform mouth-to-mouth (now called *rescue breathing*)—just maintain an open airway.

4. Open the infant's airway by placing one hand on the forehead and the other hand under the chin. Tilt the head back gently. Be sure you do not over-extend

the neck, which can cause a blocked airway. *Look, Listen,* and *Feel* for breathing again. If opening the airway did not produce breathing, begin rescue breathing immediately.

5. To perform rescue breathing, cover both the infant's nose and mouth with your mouth, getting a good seal. The breath you deliver should be a gentle "puff" lasting 1½ to 2 seconds. After each breath, remove your mouth from the infant's to allow a normal exhale. After giving two breaths, and seeing the chest rise, check the infant's pulse.

6. Check the pulse on the inside of the infant's arm halfway between the elbow and shoulder using your index finger and middle finger. Check for 5 to 10 seconds.

If Pulse Is Felt:

1. DO NOT perform chest compressions.

2. Give one breath every 3 seconds.

3. Check pulse every 20 breaths.

Continue rescue breathing until help arrives or until the infant begins breathing again.

If Pulse Is Absent:

1. Begin chest compressions by placing your middle and ring finger on the sternum one finger's width below the nipple line. Depress chest half an inch to 1 inch.

2. Give two quick compressions every second to imitate the infant's fast heart rate. Count compressions aloud to keep rhythm.

3. Give one breath after every five compressions.

4. Check pulse after 1 minute of compressions and rescue breathing. Continue to check pulse every few minutes.

5. Continue compressions and rescue breathing until the infant revives or help arrives.

If you are able to revive the infant, seek immediate medical treatment as soon as possible.

These instructions are a good first step on how to learn infant CPR. But like I said, to really know what you're doing, you need to take an accredited class. You can look in your local phone book to find a school or hospital that offers one or you can go online to get your certification. Two websites to check out are www.emergencyuniversity.com and www.FirstAidWeb.com.

To me, however, the one method that really stands out is an in-home course through the Red Cross. In roughly the time it takes to watch the Super Bowl, minus the pregame preamble, a certified Red Cross instructor will come to your house and teach you and up to 11 adults how to perform adult, child, and infant CPR, as well as first aid for choking. You'll get personal instruction, watch a video, get practice on training mannequins, and receive resource materials for emergencies. The cost? About the same as taking an out-of-home class, approximately $25 to $40 per person, depending on where you live. Call the Red Cross or log on to www.redcross.org for details.

If you're a new dad or an expectant dad, don't hesitate. Learn infant CPR ASAP.

"I'm going to call the Red Cross right now."

"I'm going to call the Red Cross right— wait a minute, the game's on."

GOOD DAD

BAD DAD

5

DON'T
PUT A
"BABY ON BOARD"
SIGN IN YOUR
CAR WINDOW

I know they've been around for years, but putting one of these signs in your car window doesn't tell the world you're a caring father, it tells the world you have no cojónes … I mean it, nerd-boy. And if your wife is the one who made you do it, that's even worse!

I never understood those signs anyway. Just because you have a child in your car doesn't mean I'm going to drive any safer around you. In the first place, I'm a watchful, considerate driver no matter who or what you're transporting. Children, chickens, it makes no difference.

FATHER FIGURE

Estimated number of dads in the United States: 66.3 million

Second, I resent the fact that what you're telling me is, basically, I'm a reckless maniac behind the wheel and that I need to be more vigilant around you because of your "cargo." Well you know what? I probably have my kids in my car and I'll be driving cautiously because that's what you're supposed to do.

By the way, having one of those signs in your car does not give you the right to drive below the speed limit. Go with the flow of traffic and stop being an impediment to other drivers who are observing the law. People who drive slower than the speed limit are a road hazard. Period.

So get on-board, baby. Those signs are nothing more than a shallow, outward attempt to tell others what a great parent you are. And if you truly are the Good Dad, people already know that … by the way you drive, and otherwise.

"Sign? I don't need no stinking sign."

"I'll take two, one for each minivan."

GOOD DAD

BAD DAD

6

DON'T
BE AFRAID
TO SPANK

Let me preface this chapter with a joke, if I may ...

"Daddy, can I have a glass of water?"

"No, go to sleep."

"Daddy, can I have a glass of water?"

"I said no, go to sleep."

"Daddy, can I have a glass of water?"

"I said no, and if you ask me again I'm going to come in there and spank you!"

"Daddy, when you come in to spank me, can you bring me a glass of water?"

I know this chapter goes against the tide of conventional wisdom, but, in my opinion, a dad's gotta do what a dad's gotta do. And if that means spanking, then by all means, spank.

But let me make one point crystal clear: when I say spank, I'm talking a swat on the butt with an open hand, not a "whuppin'." No switches. No belts. No paddles. Nothing even remotely close. Because your goal is to get their attention and to express displeasure at their behavior, not to inflict pain or shame.

You know that expression, "This is gonna hurt me a lot more than it's gonna hurt you?" I never fully understood the truth in that statement until I spanked my oldest son for the first time. Afterward, I felt *terrible*. To this day, if I swat my kids, I feel bad. But with my two boys, sometimes spanking is the only way to make them listen.

To that point, when it comes to discipline, you must exercise precise reason and judgment, and tailor it for each child. Some children are very sensitive and the act of spanking would be detrimental rather than beneficial. If that's the case, don't do it. For example, a friend of mine has a little girl who is very sweet and obedient, but when she does something that requires disciplinary measures, his raised voice almost brings her to tears. Needless to say, spanking would not be the best way to handle her, and he's never had to.

However, when I was a small boy, if I did something that went against what my mom wanted me to do, I got spanked. Sometimes I'd run from her and hide under the bed, where she couldn't reach me. But once—man oh man, was she mad. I don't even remember what I did, but she chased me and I, of course, went straight to the safe confines under my bed. For the first time ever, and much to my surprise, she physically moved—by herself mind you—my heavy, wooden double-bed; found me hiding underneath; pulled me out by my ankles; and proceeded to dole out her version of corporal punishment. Every angry word uttered from my usually loving, caring mother was punctuated with a well-placed swat on my butt. It went something like this: "Don't ... *thwack* ... you ... *thwack* ... ever ... *thwack* ... do ... *thwack* ... that ... *thwack* ... again!"

Whoa. I couldn't believe the person who birthed me, nurtured me, and taught me right from wrong could get that mad at me. Me! Her only son! But she did. The spanking didn't even hurt; I was more surprised than anything. And guess what? I never did it again—whatever it was—and it was the spanking that got my attention.

Don't spank routinely, either. Save it for the really naughty stuff. It's like swearing. If you consistently pepper your adult conversations with curse words, it dilutes the meaning of those words and they lose their punch. But if you rarely swear and, on occasion, make a point with a strategically placed curse word—believe me, you'll get people's attention. Same goes with a smack on the behind. A little goes a long way.

Now, it would be remiss of me not to mention other forms of discipline that should be tried before you resort to spanking. Sitting down and talking is always an option, but the child needs to be old enough to understand what you are trying to get across. Then there's the ubiquitous timeout. You know, sending the child to their room or wherever to spend a few minutes alone to think about what they've done. People who study this stuff recommend a minute for every year of age. For example, a 4-year-old should be given a timeout for no longer than 4 minutes. A 5-year-old, 5 minutes. And so on. You can also take away a favorite toy, book, or other object that is very important to the child. In my experience, this works well.

In the end, spanking should be used as a last resort, and sparingly. But I truly believe that with certain kids, there's a direct anatomical connection between their butt and their ears.

"This is gonna hurt me a lot more than it's gonna hurt you."

"Awright, where's my can of whup-ass?"

GOOD DAD

BAD DAD

7

GIVE LOTS OF HORSY, PIGGYBACK, AND SHOULDER RIDES

What do you want, a pie chart? Kids love 'em. Enough said.

*"Saddle up,
let's ride!"*

*"Not tonight, kids,
my [insert body part
here] is killing me."*

GOOD DAD

BAD DAD

8

GET
LIFE INSURANCE

I hear dads all the time making excuses why they don't have life insurance.

"It's too expensive."

"It's too complicated."

"I don't trust insurance salesmen."

Whimper, whimper, whimper. If you're one of these guys, I'm here to tell you to stop your whining. Be the Good Dad and do your research, find a good company, lock in the premium that's right for you and buy it.

As "dad," you're probably the head of the household when it comes to providing for the family financially. Even if your wife works, odds are you make more money. (If she makes more than you, atta-boy.) As the breadwinner, your wife and children are dependent on you. If you're gone, so is your income. How is your wife supposed to cover the mortgage, the groceries, clothes, college funds, and so on, and so on, with no money?

One reason people think shopping for life insurance is so complicated is that there are so many choices. Not just the sheer volume of life insurance companies but the number and type of policies. Whole Life. Variable Life. Universal Life. I'm here to make it really easy for you: don't buy anything except Term Life Insurance. That's it. You don't need anything else. Those other policies are called "Cash Value." Apparently "value" is a relative term because they definitely are *not* a value, they're expensive and come with all sorts of extras you don't need, such as an investment feature. Don't let an agent snow you. Get Term Life. End of story.

Term Life is exactly what it sounds like. You're covered—and your family is protected—for a certain length of time, a term. Ten years? Twenty years? Depends. How old are your kids? How long will they be dependent on you and your income? If they're teenagers, a 20-year policy is kind of silly because they'll be on their own fairly soon. Got a newborn? Ten years isn't enough. Simply think it through.

Now the question remains; how much? A rule of thumb is 10 times your annual income. Some people recommend 20 times your annual income, which is a pretty big nut, but if you can afford it, go for it.

Speaking of being able to afford it, shop around. Different insurance companies have different prices for the same policy. I wouldn't go the ultra-cheap route, however. Go with a known, reputable company with a proven track record, not some fly-by-night insurance company that may not be around in 5 years.

Want to save even more money? Get life insurance while you're young and healthy. After age 40, things get pricier. Plus, the older you get, the more things can go wrong with your health. If you develop diabetes or a heart condition, that can send your costs through the roof. Do you smoke? Stop. That'll help you out in more ways than one.

Insurance companies can be sneaky, too, so you have to watch your back. Pay in full, not in "convenient monthly payments." Why? Because some companies charge extra for this so-called convenience—sometimes the fees can be 20 percent of your annual premium. And they bury them in the total cost, so you don't even know you're paying for them. (Bastards.)

Also, if your wife is a stay-at-home mom and the primary caregiver, you'll want to get insurance on her too, because if something were to happen to her, you'll need money for all those extra childcare costs.

Speaking of children, don't ever get insurance on your kids, unless they make more money than you and you depend on *their* income. This probably happens more in Hollywood than Topeka, but hey, it happens. T'ain't worth it.

So you see, life insurance isn't scary. You dying *without* life insurance, that's scary.

"The peace of mind is well worth the cost."

"Don't need it, I'm healthy as a horse. Ow, what was that?"

GOOD DAD

BAD DAD

9

DO

TAKE LOTS
OF PICTURES

Quick. What's the one thing, besides family members and pets, that most people would run into a burning house to save? That's right, pictures. Those precious, priceless, once-in-a-lifetime moments frozen in time. That's why you need to take pictures. Lots of them. It's that important.

Put them in an album. Keep them on a disc. Stash them in a box. Store them on your hard drive. Whatever you do, just take them. Snap away with reckless abandon, otherwise you'll have no visual history chronicling your children's lives and there's *no* way of going back. Ever.

Waiting for that perfect photo op? Don't. You can mine for gold in the simplest situations—not just birthdays, graduations, weddings, and other major events.

When it comes to taking pictures, do you have a tendency to cut off your subjects' heads or make the picture look like you shot it during an earthquake? No worries. Today's auto-focus 35mm and digital cameras are pretty idiot-proof, so you no longer have to share the same bloodline as Ansel Adams to take good pictures. But there are a few fundamental rules to help you take even better ones. Here are a few courtesy of Kodak.com:

- **Look your subject in the eye.** Direct eye contact can be as engaging in a picture as it is in real life.

- **Use a plain background.** A plain background shows off the subject you're photographing. Also, make sure no poles grow from the head of your favorite niece and that no cars dangle from her ears.

- **Use a flash outdoors.** Bright sun can create unattractive deep facial shadows. Eliminate the shadows by using your flash to lighten your subject.

- **Move in closer.** Take a step or two closer to your subject. Your goal is to fill the picture area with the subject to create pictures with greater impact. But don't get too close or your pictures will be blurry.

- **Move your subject from the middle.** Center-stage is a great place for a performer, but not your subject. Bring your picture to life by simply moving your subject away from the middle of your picture.

- **Take candid pictures.** Ignore the impulse to force your subjects to always pose staring at the camera. Show them playing, chatting, or relaxing.

- **Begin a photo tradition.** Take pictures regularly so that you, your family, and friends can see how much your child has changed. Capture your child setting off for the first day of school each year. Or mark your child's growth against a tree as you watch your child and the tree grow. Or every Father's Day, surround Granddad with the grandkids.

One thing to keep in mind: make sure you get yourself in the pictures. One day I was leafing through several of our photo albums when I noticed something was missing. Me. There were tons of pictures of my wife and kids, but where was I? Always behind the camera. Don't be shy to hand it off to a relative, your wife, or your kids and have them snap away. Better yet use the self-timer, that way everybody gets in the picture, even dear ol' dad. And it's one way, albeit a humbling one, to keep tabs on that receding hairline.

One thing we've had a lot of luck with is making a calendar out of the best snapshots we've taken throughout the year. They make great holiday presents for the grandparents, aunts, uncles, or anyone else who loves to grace their walls with the adorable, smiling faces of your children.

Do you own a camcorder? Then take as many videos as you can, too. A good healthy mix of stills and video is a great way to document the passage of time. Digital camcorders are gaining popularity, but I'm sure a lot of you have a library of standard 8mm tapes stashed in drawers or boxes. If so, you might want to think of transferring them onto a DVD. They keep better that way. Look in the phone book and I'm sure you'll find a place or two able to do the transfer for you.

As they say, every picture tells a story. And Good Dads have lots of "stories" to tell about their children.

"Okay everybody, say 'Cheese!'"

"I thought YOU brought the camera!"

GOOD DAD

BAD DAD

10

DON'T
BE OBVIOUS WITH
YOUR BAD HABITS

Warning: Keep out of reach of children. This is the label that should be slapped on your forehead every time you indulge a bad habit. Do you read men's magazines? Do you @#%*!§‡ swear? (And you kiss your kids with that mouth?) Do you drink a six-pack of soda a day? Do you listen to music with explicit lyrics?

That's fine, we all have our vices. But do be discreet, especially as your kids get older. Having a bad habit doesn't necessarily mean you're a Bad Dad, it just means that you're human. Every person on this planet has some little peccadillo they're not too proud of. You don't lapse into Bad Dad territory just because you, say, binge on junk food occasionally.

But where things get a little fuzzy and the boundaries blur is if your children find out about your bad habit and emulate it, or even worse, you let your bad habit be a detriment to the kids or the family unit as a whole. For example, I recently read that 60 percent of American adults are overweight, and 30 percent of children. The result is an epidemic of "adult-onset" Type-2 diabetes in children. Something to think about the next time you have your arms full of Twinkies, Ho-Hos, and Pringles.

Kids are sponges. They absorb everything they see and hear, especially if it comes from you. They love you and look up to you and identity with you wholeheartedly—until they're teenagers, anyway—and if they observe you performing some sort of behavioral impropriety they'll think it's okay because daddy does it. Monkey see, monkey do. So make sure you do the right thing, my simian friend. Lead by example.

▬▬▬ FATHER FIGURE ▬▬▬

Estimated number of sporting goods stores in the United States: 22,410

Unfortunately, we live in an R-rated world. Turn on MTV or HBO and you'll see and hear things that would make a sailor blush. Look, I'm no prude. I've had my share of indiscretions and I'm sure you have, too. But, good or bad, I found them out on my own; I didn't learn them from my parents. Older siblings? Sure. Friends? Oh, yeah. But mom or dad? Not a chance. Which is the way it should be.

Your kids will grow up soon enough and find out about all the senseless, unhealthy, and yes, stupid stuff that grown-ups do to themselves and others. Don't you want your children to hang on to that beautiful childhood innocence as long as possible? Of course you do. So why expose them to adult foibles, especially yours, before they're ready?

One last thing: if you smoke cigarettes, check out Chapter 13, which I devote solely to this habit. Yes, it deserves one.

To summarize, bad habits don't make Bad Dads. But being discreet about bad habits, thus being a Good Dad, can be very habit-forming.

"The kids are sound asleep, think I'll check out Miss July."

"No, no, Brandon— when Daddy said, 'Look at the pair on her,' I meant her feet."

GOOD DAD   **BAD DAD**

11

DO

CREATE A FAMILY DISASTER PLAN

Blizzards, floods, ice storms, mudslides, tidal surges … when it comes to natural disasters, America certainly has its fair share. Hurricanes march across Florida. Tornadoes rip through Kansas. Earthquakes rattle California. Wildfires devastate Colorado. No matter where you live, there's a natural disaster just waiting to happen. Post-9/11, we now have to worry about man-made disasters such as explosions. Scary.

As a Good Dad, you're obviously concerned about your family's safety and welfare. That's why it's imperative you create a *Family Disaster Plan*, a detailed plan that spells out what to do if disaster strikes: how to evacuate, where to meet, who to call—things such as that.

I know, I know, it's one of those things you don't want to think about. It's easy to lapse into *laissez faire*, shrug off the worry, and dispel it with a defiant, "It won't happen to me." Don't be naïve. It *can* happen to you. And having that type of attitude is quite a gamble, considering you're betting with the lives of your children.

Another easy excuse is, "That's why I pay taxes … for fire, police, and such." True. But when hundreds, thousands, perhaps tens of thousands of people are all trying to get through to 911, there might be a slight delay in response time to your personal request.

What's the Boy Scout motto? Be prepared. Well, guess what, it's now the official Good Dad motto. Be prepared for an emergency and you could save the lives of not only your family, but your neighbors and others as well.

Here in California, with all the disasters we're subjected to year in and year out, we have what's called the Governor's Office of Emergency Services. I'm sure your state has something similar. On their website, www.oes.ca.gov, they offer tips on how to plan and prepare your family for an emergency, including:

- Stocking up on at least a 3-day supply of food, water, clothes, medical supplies, and other necessary equipment for everyone in your family.

- Deciding where and when to reunite your family should you be apart when a disaster strikes.

- Choosing a person outside the immediate area to contact if family members are separated. Long distance phone service will probably be restored sooner than local service. Do not use the phone immediately after a major emergency.

- Locating the shut-off valves for water, gas, and electricity. Learn how to shut off the valves before an emergency. If you have any questions, call your utility company.

- Making copies of vital records and keeping them in a safe deposit box in another city or state. Make sure your originals are stored safely.

- Establishing all the possible ways to exit your house. Keep those areas clear.

- Knowing the locations of the nearest fire and police stations.

- Taking photos/videos of your valuables. Making copies and keeping them with a friend or relative in another city or state.

- Keeping an extra pair of eyeglasses and house and car keys on hand.

- Keeping extra cash and change in a secure, easily-accessible place, such as a fireproof household safe. If electricity is out, you will not be able to use an ATM.

These tips are the tip of the natural-disaster iceberg. (If you live in Alaska or any of the polar regions, you can take that last statement literally.) There's so much more to cover, but this is a good start. Do a little research on your own and I'm sure you'll find some specific rules and guidelines that pertain to your state or community.

All Good Dads, take heed: be prepared. Because if you're not, *that* could spell disaster.

"Water? Check. Food? Check. Medical supplies? Check ..."

"What, me worry?"

GOOD DAD

BAD DAD

12

DO

KISS YOUR WIFE GOODBYE IN THE MORNING, AND KISS HER HELLO WHEN YOU COME HOME

Easy enough, right? A smooch on the lips. A peck on the cheek. Well, you wouldn't believe how many guys don't perform this simple ritual. "What," I hear you asking, "does this have to do with being a Good Dad?"

Plenty. Being a Good Dad means setting a good example, no matter what the circumstances. Seeing Mommy and Daddy sharing this brief but tender moment shows the boys how a man should act toward his wife, and it shows the girls how a husband should treat a woman.

Okay, now that you know osculation (look it up) is more than a precursor to a "happy ending," lodge this next point somewhere deep inside your gray matter, too: no matter what your feelings toward your wife are at the time, it behooves you, the kids, and marital harmony to find the .03 seconds to perform this humble gesture. Are you mad at her for forgetting to change the oil in the minivan every 3,000 miles? Are you one of those guys who feels uncomfortable with public displays of affection? Tough. Suck it up and pucker up.

In the end, kissing your wife goodbye and hello reinforces the matrimonial bond. More importantly, it reinforces the bond between children and parents.* To you, it's a small gesture. To them, it's a sense of security. And a feeling of security from both Mom and Dad is major for children.

Bottom line: get on the buss, and never step off.

"Bye, hon [smooch]. See you tonight!"

"Sorry, hon, gotta run."

GOOD DAD   **BAD DAD**

(*Don't make the kiss too passionate, Romeo. Stick to the basics. You want to nurture your kids, not gross 'em out.)

13

DO QUIT SMOKING

A no-brainer, right? Then for all you dads out there who still smoke, I pose this question: why haven't you quit?

Don't worry, I'm not going to lecture you on the dangers of smoking. You know all about the heart disease, the emphysema, the strokes, the lung cancers, the mouth cancers, yada yada yada. If you want to slowly and systematically kill yourself, go right ahead—this is a free country and I can't make you quit.

But don't kill your kids. As you may or may not know, secondhand smoke is nearly as dangerous as putting those cancer sticks into your kids' mouths and having them inhale the scorching, carcinogenic ash into their virgin lungs themselves.

According to the American Lung Association, children who breathe second-hand smoke are more likely to suffer from pneumonia, bronchitis, and other lung diseases. They have more ear infections and are more likely to develop asthma. If they do have asthma, they suffer more attacks. Plus, there are an estimated 150,000 to 300,000 cases every year of infections such as bronchitis and pneumonia in infants and children under 18 months of age who breathe secondhand smoke. This results in between 7,500 and 15,000 hospitalizations.

If that's not enough, secondhand smoke causes approximately 3,000 deaths each year from lung cancer in people who don't smoke, and approximately 35,000 deaths per year from heart disease. Again, in people who don't smoke.

Now, I know some dads reading this are saying, "No worries, I step outside and smoke." That's a good move, but not good enough. You still smoke. Your kids still see you smoke. They still smell it on your breath and on your clothes. And if you smoke, odds are your children will smoke, and they'll grow up facing the same grim consequences every smoker does. Believe it or not, children start experimenting with cigarettes around 8 or 9 years of age. Plus, kids who smoke are more likely to experiment with alcohol, marijuana, cocaine, and other illicit drugs. You don't want that for your children, do you? Of course not—no Good Dad does.

But here's the good news. New research suggests that quitting smoking before your children turn 8, or enter third grade, reduces the chance of your kids smoking in their teens by 39 percent. How's that for motivation? The best protection, of course, is for kids to come from a family where both parents never smoked. In that case, children are 71 percent less likely to become smokers.

There is one catch to all this, however. You have to quit. Therein lies the problem. Tobacco companies aren't stupid. Evil, yes, but not stupid. They've known for years that nicotine is as addictive as heroin and that it's extremely difficult to kick the habit. So if you need that extra push to quit—and a lot of people do—you need a 3-point game plan of counseling, social support, and maybe OTC medications such as nicotine gum or patches. But don't take my word as gospel. Point your cursor in the direction of these websites and they can help you out: anti-smoking.org, lungusa.org, and americanlegacy.com.

Chew instead of smoke? Practically just as bad. Same chemicals, same poisons, same dangers. No secondhand smoke, but the "monkey see, monkey do" factor is still there.

The dangers of smoking cigarettes, pipes, and cigars are well documented. But now that you have kids, it's no longer just about you. So for your own good—and especially your kids—stop smoking.

End of sermon. You may now move on to the next chapter.

"That's it,
I'm quitting."

"I've quit before,
I can do it again."

GOOD DAD

BAD DAD

14

DON'T
BE THE
BAD SPORTS DAD

Tempers flare. Expletives fly. Fists connect. Noses break. Professional wrestling on late-night cable? Nah. Just another typical day at your kids' baseball game. Or hockey game. Or soccer game. Surprisingly—or not so surprisingly—the hooligans who start these melees are not the prepubescent athletes. They're the parents. The drive to be #1 is becoming so important to this pack of misguided idiots that they're neglecting their #1 priority: the health and welfare of their children.

We've all read the stories about sports parents who have actually assaulted officials, even their own team's coaches, for the most ludicrous of reasons— supposed bad calls or not starting their son or daughter, to name a few. What are these people thinking? When did violence become the accepted way to behave? Having your child play youth baseball, sixth-grade football, or varsity basketball is supposed to help them acquire new skills, learn good sportsmanship, and have fun, not learn how to act like a first-class jerk—much less a felon. If your kids see you take a swing at a referee or coach, they're going to think it's okay to settle their own scores with violence. Not good.

The crisis has gotten so out of hand that many communities and states are initiating programs to help change the way schools, coaches, and parents approach children's sports programs. The University of Maine even launched a statewide project called Sports Done Right. Log on to their website at www. sportsdonerightmaine.org and you'll find suggestions on how to be a Good Sports Dad, including:

- Encouraging your child, regardless of his or her degree of success or level of skill.

- Ensuring a balance in your student athlete's life—encouraging participation in multiple sports and activities while placing academics first.

- Emphasizing enjoyment, development of skills, and team play as the cornerstones of your child's early sports experiences while reserving serious competition for the varsity level.

- Leaving coaching to coaches and avoiding placing too much pressure on your youngster about playing time and performance.

- Being realistic about your child's future in sports— recognize that only a select few earn a college scholarship, compete in the Olympics, or sign a professional contract.

- Being there when your child looks to the sidelines for a positive role model.

Do dads who flip out, scream, use coarse language, and behave poorly love their children? Absolutely. Are they prime examples of Bad Dads? Absolutely.

So don't do it.

"It's not whether you win or lose, it's how you play the game."

"#@#$%!*!%$@#!!!"*

GOOD DAD   **BAD DAD**

15

DO

LEARN HOW TO MAKE FRUIT SMOOTHIES

That's right, fruit smoothies. They're easy, they're delicious, they're healthy, and kids love 'em. What more could you ask for?

Here's our story. My wife, to her credit, always tried to feed our kids fruit and other nutritious food items. But it was exasperating: one day they liked something, the next day they didn't. Then one day after the gym I stopped at one of those smoothie places, got myself a jumbo, and came home. One of the boys, who was pretty young at the time, probably 3, was very curious about the gigantic, multicolored cup I had in my hand. He looked inside at the contents and wanted a taste. (I think he thought it was ice cream.) So I gave him a small spoonful. I'm tellin' you, the look on that kid's face was like he just tasted manna from heaven. He ended up drinking most of it. Bing! The proverbial light went on. So I started making them myself, and my kids have been drinking them ever since.

What I usually do is whip up a batch for breakfast, especially before we go someplace I know the kids will be gorging themselves on junk food—birthday parties, county fairs, professional sporting events, stuff like that. That way they at least start the day with a nutritious meal and I don't feel as guilty when I see them downing their third hot dog or diving headfirst into a bowl of chips. Smoothies for lunch or dinner? Sure, why not? Nobody's stopping you.

The following is my own smoothie recipe that is as delicious as it is easy.

FRUIT SMOOTHIE

In a standard blender (that's right, the same kind you use for those killer margaritas), toss in:

1 banana	*1 (6-oz.) container vanilla*
1/2 can crushed pineapple	*yogurt*
1/2 cup fresh strawberries	*2 cups orange juice*
(frozen will work)	*Squeeze of honey*
	Handful of ice

Blend 'til smooth

This recipe will feed roughly 2 to 3 toddlers, 1 to 2 tweens, or 1 teen. You can vary this recipe in a number of ways—experimenting with the ingredients is half the fun. For example, use cranberry juice instead of orange juice. Blueberries instead of strawberries. Lemon yogurt, more bananas, no pineapple, fresh oranges, canned peaches, coconut, whatever your heart and taste buds desire. Some people use milk.

Getting the kids involved is a kick, too. Have them peel the bananas, squeeze the honey, flip the switch on the blender, whatever. Always be there to supervise them, of course. You don't want macerated fruit all over your new ceiling fan.

So there you have it, guys. Fruit smoothies, one of the best weapons in the arsenal against junk food. They're easy to make. They're healthy. And they won't pack on the pounds like fast food.

BTW: If you can't see your shoes when you stand up, maybe you should try one yourself. You'll thank me later.

"Okay, who wants a fruit smoothie?"

"Okay, who wants Froot Loops?"

GOOD DAD

BAD DAD

16

DO

MAKE YOUR KIDS' FIRST PROFESSIONAL SPORTING EVENT A MAJOR LEAGUE BASEBALL GAME

It could be football. Or basketball. Or hockey. Or even NASCAR. But in my opinion, there's a special connection between kids and dads and baseball that other professional sports just don't have.

I'm not sure if it's the outdoors, the time of year, the possibility of catching a foul ball, or what, but baseball seems to kick up the level of nostalgia a couple notches, adding to the whole bonding process. Besides, virtually every kid plays baseball. It's the one sport everybody can participate in.

When you think about it, baseball is more than America's Pastime, it's America itself. It's a diamond that sparkles red, white, and blue. There's even a song about it—"Take Me Out to the Ballgame." I guarantee if you sing that song loud and proud—and no doubt off-key—you won't care if you ever get back.

All this talk of baseball reminds me of the famous George Carlin routine where he compares baseball's easygoing, Andy Williams-in-a-cardigan style versus football's in-your-face, kill-the-other-guy mentality. Point being, there's a bucolic, almost idyllic nature to baseball. Very folksy. It's the comfort food of sports. The slower pace is more conducive to conversation, too, allowing you to actually talk with your child.

I'll never forget the first time I took my then 5-year-old to see his first baseball game. It was the dog days of summer, muggy and hot, and the seats were so high they gave me altitude sickness, but we had a great time anyway, eating and drinking every sugar-infused food and beverage that passed our way. Did he understand what was going on down on the field? Nah. Did it matter? Nah.

Halfway through his second billowy stick of glow-in-the-dark, pink cotton candy, there was a natural lull in the conversation and the game. At that point, he turned to me and asked, "Daddy, are there some kids who don't have daddies?" I replied yes and left it at that, not wanting to bring up my dad, who died at age 45, when I was 3 months old. He paused for a second, then wrapped his small arms around me and gave me a hug that almost cracked a rib. He then said, "I'm glad I have a daddy." Oh. My. God. Tickets to the game: $30. Cotton candy: $10. The cost of hearing him say that to me: priceless.

Like I said, if you want football, go with football. If you're into synchronized swimming, hey, I'm not going to stop you. (But someone should.) There's just something special about America's Pastime that turns every father into America's Favorite Dad.

"Grab your mitt, let's go!"

"Look! Two tickets to the World Series of Curling! Happy birthday!"

GOOD DAD

BAD DAD

17

BUY ORGANIC FOODS WHENEVER POSSIBLE

No, I don't hug trees or burn incense. I don't live in a commune, wear patchouli oil, drive a '67 VW bus, or have a child named "Moonbeam." What I am is a concerned father, a Good Dad, trying to protect my children from harm any way possible. And one way is by buying organic foods.

In case you've been living under a rock for the past 40 years, organic foods are loosely defined as any food product grown, raised, or processed without the use of synthetic fertilizers, pesticides, or other chemicals. Luckily you no longer have to wear Birkenstocks or love beads to know where to get organic items, because organic food has gone mainstream. And for good reason: consumers, scientists, even the federal government have all realized that spraying pesticides on food actually does more harm than good. Especially to children.

Recent research suggests that the residue from pesticides can harm a child's developing nervous system. And, yes, pesticides from the food we eat can accumulate in the human body, and at a rather rapid rate, too. Get this: a team of health scientists conducted a 15-day research project on elementary children. For the first 3 days, and the last 7 days, the kids ate conventional, nonorganic food. But during the middle 5 days, they switched to organic food. Fruits, vegetables, juices, cereals, and pastas. Guess what? Two common pesticides—malathion and chlorpyrifos—virtually disappeared from their systems when they switched to organic foods. On average, the children reduced their malathion levels to zero. *Zero*. And when they returned to their regular diet? The levels spiked. One child's malathion level rocketed to 263 parts per billion. Think about that. From 0 to 263 parts per billion. In a matter of days! Just from what they ate! To me, that's shocking. We literally are what we eat, and if we eat pesticide-tainted foods, we'll have pesticide-tainted bodies. And so will our children.

My wife and I have switched to milk that doesn't contain the bovine-growth hormone rbST, and we buy organic produce, but there are a variety of other organic foods out there too. Juices, eggs, cheese, meats, peanut butter, ketchup, and even wheat- and corn-based items such as cereal and pasta are organic. And don't be fooled by the word "natural" either. The words "natural" and "organic" are not interchangeable.

Unfortunately, organic foods are harder to find and usually about 5 to 20 percent more expensive. Which raises the question: how do you protect your children from pesticides if you don't have access to organic foods or you honestly can't afford to purchase them?

If you have to buy conventional produce, wash it thoroughly and peel the skins. Steer completely clear of the items that have been found to have the most residue: peaches, apples, pears, grapes, green beans, spinach, winter squash, strawberries, and cantaloupe. The lowest levels of residue? Bananas, broccoli, canned peaches, canned or frozen corn, milk, orange juice, apple juice, and grape juice.

As the Good Dad, armed with all this new information, you now know what to do: break out the lava lamp, hang some black light posters, and throw on *In-A-Gadda-Da-Vida*—you're going organic.

Peace, man.

"Organic, here we come!"

"Honey, it says here we need to go orgasmic. I'm all for that!"

GOOD DAD   **BAD DAD**

18

DON'T
GET A MINIVAN

You may be a dad, but you're still a guy. Minivan: mini *man*. Need I say more?

"Check out my new all-wheel-drive sport wagon. Plenty of room for the kids, plenty of fun for me."

GOOD DAD

"Check it out— 24 cup holders!"

BAD DAD

19

LEARN HOW TO MASTER AT LEAST ONE DISH

You don't have to take lessons at some fancy cooking school, but you should, at the very least, master one dish. This gives your wife a much-needed break from the kitchen, and it teaches the kids that dads do mom things, too.

Think throwing a couple steaks on the grill is "cooking"? Sorry, guys. Grilling is a man's domain in the first place. It involves meat, roaring flames, and a hint of danger—that's why we're so attracted to it. Manning the grill makes us feel, well, manly—providing for the family in the face of peril. So, no, grilling doesn't count.

I'm talking about a dish or meal that involves peeling, chopping, slicing, dicing, browning, sautéing, simmering, frying, or baking. Preferably indoors. Your new signature dish can be easy or as complicated as you want, but why put added pressure on yourself? Take the path of least resistance and find something you can actually make. If you don't know your aspic from a hole in the ground, don't choose something such as Coquilles Saint-Jacques or duck a l'orange. That's just crazy talk.

Now, Wolfgang Puck I am not. I've tried to cook many times and failed miserably. Too salty. Too soggy. Too tasteless. Too burnt. However, I didn't give up. I wanted a dish I could call my own, so I persevered and found one. It's a dish my father used to make on Sundays. It fed the whole family, but more importantly, it fed my mom's need to just kick back and relax. It's an eastern European chicken and rice recipe called Tava. It's easy. It's delicious. And here it is:

TAVA

Chicken thighs (2 per adult)	1 (8-oz.) can stewed tomatoes
2 cups rice	1–2 cans chicken broth
1–2 chopped onions	Olive oil
5 carrots (¾ lb.)	Butter
2 TB. paprika	Salt and pepper to taste

Peel and cut carrots and parboil for 10 min. Set aside. Brown chicken pieces in olive oil skin-side down and set aside. Drain fat. In same pan, sauté onions in olive oil and butter until translucent. Rinse the rice and put in same pan with the onions, drippings, and so on, and stir until coated. Turn off heat and add the paprika (apparently paprika can burn) mixing everything together. Put rice mixture in 9×13 baking dish, place carrots in the mixture, and cover rice with the stewed tomatoes (crush with hands, but watch your clothing because they squirt). Place chicken in pan on top of rice mixture, then pour the chicken broth to cover rice completely. Cook for 1½ hours at 375°F.

(Check rice around an hour. You may need to take the chicken out and stir the rice to make sure it's cooking thoroughly, not crunchy. If needed, add more broth. You might want to baste the chicken with juices as well.)

Tava is my signature dish; the one I make all the time for the entire family. However, the first dish I attempted that actually was table-worthy was Linguine and Clams. Talk about easy. From start to finish, 20 minutes. And it tastes like it's from a restaurant. No lie. Here, have at it:

LINGUINE AND CLAMS

1 package linguine

3 cans clams (1 chopped, 2 minced)

Garlic (4 cloves, sliced)

Green onion (2, sliced)

Italian parsley (handful, chopped)

Red pepper flakes to taste

½ lemon

Butter

Olive oil

2 splashes of wine (one for the dish, one for the cook!)

Boil a pot of water for the linguine. When boiling, throw the pasta in and cook about 8 minutes or until al dente; drain and set aside. Put butter and olive oil in pan, sauté garlic and green onion until garlic turns translucent, but don't burn. Then throw in the clams, juice and all. Throw in Italian parsley, red pepper flakes, and splash of wine. Let simmer 5 minutes. Turn off heat, squeeze juice of half a lemon into dish (make sure you don't get any seeds in there), and toss with the linguine.

Admittedly, the younger kids aren't too wild about this dish, what with the garlic and onions and all, but older kids like it. The Mrs. will definitely love it. Here's an idea: the next time you find yourselves alone in the house, have a nice romantic dinner in. I guarantee if you make your wife this dish, complemented by candles and a nice chilled bottle of Chardonnay, you can be assured of extending your amorous evening well into the night, if you catch my drift.

There you go, fellas. Two dishes you can call your own, straight from the *Good Dad/Bad Dad* cookbook. Your wife will thank you. Your children will love you. What more could you want from life?

"*Bon appetit, everyone.*"

"*More SpaghettiOs, anyone?*"

GOOD DAD

BAD DAD

20

DON'T

FALL FOR THE "5-SECOND RULE"

You're familiar with the 5-Second Rule, right? It states that if a piece of food falls on the floor and you pick it up within 5 seconds, it's okay to give to your child because it wasn't exposed to the germs on the floor long enough to be "dirty."

Sorry to break it to you, but the 5-Second Rule isn't a rule. It's a myth. A disgusting one at that.

Fact is, your floor is one big linoleum Petri dish. It's coated with all sorts of bacteria and germs and viruses and everything else that the cat dragged in. Whatever you stepped in outside is on your floor. Consequently, the *second* a piece of food falls on the floor it comes into contact with whatever contaminant is present at that instant in that spot. (Did you know that toilet seats are cleaner than floors?)

So, basically, there is no 5-Second Rule, fool. Two seconds, 6 seconds, 5 seconds, it's all the same: contaminated. Sure, I've used the 5-Second Rule to justify my actions. All parents do. But let's not kid ourselves. If you want to give your child a piece of food that has been on the floor for less than five seconds, fine, but don't think you're doing it out of cleanliness. You're doing it out of laziness.

Here's a thought: did your floor just get wet-mopped? It might be cleaner than one that didn't. Could the 5-Second Rule apply then? I guess it depends on your mop; it's your call. Also, I'm guesstimating that dry foods won't pick up as many microbes as the wetter, juicier ones, right? Makes sense. Keep that little nugget in the back of your mind the next time your child drops a Cheerio versus, say, a small piece of fruit.

In conclusion, there should be a new rule: *if it falls on the floor, it ain't food no more.* If you can't stick with this new rule, you'll have to deal with the knowledge that you knowingly gave your child contaminated food—which falls under the category of Bad Dad.

But hey, I won't tell anybody if you won't.

"Oops, sorry Sarah, Daddy has to throw it away."

"Oops, sorry Sarah, let Daddy wipe it off … here ya go."

GOOD DAD

BAD DAD

21

DON'T

FUND YOUR KIDS' COLLEGE EDUCATION AT THE EXPENSE OF FUNDING YOUR OWN RETIREMENT

Sounds cold-hearted, doesn't it? A prime example of Bad Dad-ness. I mean, what kind of a callous father would even think of opting for a cushy retirement over the future of his children? I'll tell you what kind: a smart one.

As the Good Dad, you've made countless sacrifices over the years for your kids. Pretty much on a daily basis. But this is one area where you can guiltlessly say, "Me first."

The reason is simple: you can always borrow money to pay for a higher education, but you'll never, ever, *ever*, get a bank to lend you money for retirement. I can see the scenario now:

"Yes, sir, may I help you?"

"You sure can: I need to take out a loan."

"Okay, great. Just let me ask you a few questions. Now, how much would you like to borrow?"

"A million would be good."

"A million? Um, may I ask what you need the money for?"

"Retirement."

"Retirement?"

"Retirement."

"I see … ahem … security!"

There are only a few ways to save for retirement, but there is an abundance of ways to pay for college. 529 plans. Low-cost student loans. Scholarships. Financial aid. Going to a less-expensive school. Heck, tell your kids to get a part-time job—they're young and healthy. You can even (gulp) have them live at home for the first couple years. Here's another way to look at this whole scenario: if you don't have enough retirement savings, *you* might be forced to live with *your* adult kids (bigger gulp).

Now, I'm not saying don't save for college, just be prudent about it and make contributions to both a college fund *and* your retirement, with your 401(k) and IRA getting top priority. Did you know that the federal financial aid formula does not—I repeat, does *not*—include the money in your retirement accounts when figuring out how much you can afford to pay for college? See how all this is making sense? Hey, and don't forget, if your company matches your 401(k) contributions, that's free money.

Ruthless? Cold-hearted? Callous? Nope: smart. Be the Good Dad and put yourself first. For once.

"We're set. And so are the kids."

GOOD DAD

"We'll be living on the street, but at least Kelsey and Brandon are going to Yale."

BAD DAD

22

GET A LOCK ON YOUR BEDROOM DOOR

Knock, knock.

No, this isn't a joke. Just a simple reminder of the sound you will never, *ever* hear before one of your kids bursts into your bedroom looking for you—no matter the time, no matter what compromising position you and your wife may be engaged in.

Hence, a door lock.

I've heard too many stories from too many dads who were in the middle of a passionate interlude when—hello—a small child wants more water or an older one wants more money. You may think the little ones are asleep, but they're not. You may think you have the house to yourselves late at night, but you don't.

Hence, a door lock.

Now, you don't have to worry so much about the teeny-tiny ones; you can make up some story, any story, and they'll probably believe you. Something with a rabbit usually works. But if you've got older kids and they see dear old dad and sweet innocent mom going at it like crazed weasels, they might need years of expensive therapy to erase that image. *Then* they'll stick *you* with the bill. You don't want that.

Hence, a door lock.

Remember the first time you heard about sexual intercourse? Remember the first time you realized that your mom and dad "did it"? It's frightening. "Mom and Dad would never do that. No way!" Yes way. Mommy and Daddy can rub uglies with the best of them. It's just something no child should ever witness.

Hence, a door lock.

I know, I know, the physical act of getting up to latch the door, which I fondly call *lockus interruptus,* can put a real damper on things when Daddy's trying to get some much-needed sugar, but it's worth the imposition. Of course, you could always be the Bad Husband and have your wife get up to lock the door, in which case, atta-boy!

While we're on the subject, you and the Mrs. might also want to—how shall I say this?—dial down the volume of your lovemaking. I heard a story about a dad who was always very careful about locking the door. Unfortunately, he was unable to curb his wife's rather audible sounds of appreciation. That is, until the day his teenage daughter confronted both of them with the shocking news that she could hear them behind closed doors. All. The. Time. There was enough embarrassment to go around for everybody.

Okay, back to the subject at hand. The moral of the story? Lock. Rhymes with *knock*. Get one, get the other.

"Why you little minx ... hang on while I lock the door."

GOOD DAD

"We woke you up? Sorry, sweetie—no, no, Mommy and Daddy were just ... ah ... wrestling. Naked ... under the covers ... with the lights off. Yes, Mommy won because she was on top. Now go back to sleep."

BAD DAD

23

DO

STRESS GOOD MANNERS AND POLITE BEHAVIOR IN YOUR CHILDREN

I'm not advocating sending your son to charm school or turning your daughter into Emily Post, but if you haven't noticed lately, common courtesy is no longer common. Manners, civility, and polite behavior have taken a back seat to crude, rude, and obnoxious behavior. Blame our fast-paced society. Blame our high-tech existence. Blame spoiled athletes and self-absorbed celebrities.

Blame parents.

According to a recent poll, 70 percent of those questioned said people are ruder than they were 20 to 30 years ago. I don't disagree. When you were a kid, do you ever remember anything remotely resembling, say, road rage? Now, of the 1,001 adults surveyed for this poll, a startling 93 percent placed the blame on … take a guess … yup, parents.

FATHER FIGURE

Number of stay-at-home dads: 147,000

As a father, I resent that. I mean, 93 percent polled placed the blame on *parents!* B.S. My wife and I have always emphasized the importance of good manners. "Please" and "thank you" and "I'm sorry" are bandied about frequently in our household, and we make sure our kids say it at every turn. In my opinion, I feel a lot of people—especially those without kids—are a little too quick to blame parents for every little thing.

However, as the Good Dad, you are the first line of defense in teaching your kids right from wrong, in all areas, including civility. Lead by example. If you don't say "please" and "thank you" and "I'm sorry," your kids won't either. And if you're the first one to honk your horn or raise your middle finger at another driver, don't be surprised when your kids do the same. Speaking of drivers acting badly, the influence of my poor driving manners became clear to me one day when my son was about 4. He was in his car seat when another driver cut in front of us. I was just about to vocalize my usual thoughts toward this cretin when I heard this tiny voice from the backseat yell, quite angrily, I might add, "Idiot!" I nearly swallowed my gum. Apparently I said it one too many times. Soon after that, I mellowed out my behind-the-wheel behavior.

Anyway, for better or worse, the world is becoming less formal. But that doesn't mean it has to become less polite. Bring back common courtesy. Start with yourself and your kids. And see where it goes from there.

Thank you.

"Always say 'please' and 'thank you.'"

GOOD DAD

"Hey, Bozo, sit on this and rotate!"

BAD DAD

24

DO

GET A FLU SHOT EVERY YEAR

"This won't hurt a bit."

For once, they're right. Flu shots are relatively painless. What really smarts, however, are the following statistics. According to the Centers for Disease Control, on average every year in the United States:

- Roughly 5 to 20 percent of the population gets the flu.

- More than 200,000 people are hospitalized due to flu complications.

- Approximately 36,000 people die from the flu.

Those most vulnerable? The old and the young.

No offense, but I'm not worried about you getting the flu. If you do, be a man and suck it up. Sure, you'll feel like death warmed over for a few days, but you'll bounce back. What does worry me is you passing it on to your kids.

Let's start from the beginning. What exactly is the flu? A really nasty virus, so antibiotics won't do you any good. And no, it's not just a bad cold. Colds generally stay in your head, but the flu makes your entire body want to yell *"Uncle!"* Add in the high fever, extreme fatigue, muscle aches, dry cough, sore throat, headache, and nasal congestion and you've got an illness that will knock you flat on your can for a week. It'll do the same to your kids, too—maybe even worse, especially if they're younger than 2 years old or have a chronic health condition such as asthma or diabetes. (More on this later.)

As the Good Dad, you don't want to give the flu to your kids, you want to get a flu shot—the single best way to prevent getting the flu. If you're allergic to eggs, you're out of luck, because the viruses used for flu shots are grown in eggs. If not, chances are you'll be fine. And don't worry about feeling achy or getting any flu-like symptoms either, because the viruses used in the flu shot are inactive. In other words, dead.

To get a shot, simply call your doctor and schedule an appointment. Some pharmacies and grocery stores offer them, too, as well as your local walk-in emergency center. A convenient way to find a flu shot is to check out www.flucliniclocator.org. Sponsored by the American Lung Association, simply type your zip code and a list of places offering shots near your home will pop up, including times, dates, and so on.

If you work for a company that offers flu shots, hallelujah, that makes getting one that much easier. If you don't, why not spearhead a movement to get your company to offer them? It's worth a shot. (Sorry, couldn't resist.)

Afraid of needles? Wimp. But if you are, there's always the flu mist nasal spray. But you must be in good health and under age 50. And unlike the flu shot, the flu mist does contain a live virus, albeit weakened, so you might experience some very minor flu symptoms, but probably not.

Okay, you and your wife are both vaccinated. Now for the kids. The flu shot is recommended for all children who are at high risk for serious complications from the flu. Included are all 6- to 23-month-olds, plus kids 2 to 18 years with heart disease, asthma or other pulmonary disorders, diabetes, immune deficiency, blood disorders, those on long-term aspirin therapy, and adolescent girls who may be pregnant during the flu season. And, of course, always, always, *always* check with their pediatrician first.

So for the sake of your kids, get a flu shot. And be thankful it's not a suppository.

"*That didn't hurt a bit.*"

"*Me? Nah, I never get sick.*"

GOOD DAD

BAD DAD

25

LEARN HOW TO BELCH THE ALPHABET

Your kids will think it's hilarious. But for God's sake, man, don't do it in front of the wife, if you know what's good for you.

FATHER FIGURE

Percentage of fathers with employed wives who were the primary caregiver for their preschooler: 20 percent

"Burp!"

"Hey, honey, look what I just taught Mia and Ryan."

GOOD DAD

BAD DAD

DON'T

EVER ASK YOUR CHILDREN HOW SCHOOL WAS

I can hear it now. All you dads out there grumbling, "What kind of an uninvolved father is this guy? How can you *not* ask your children how school was? Not interested in your children's activities? That's not just wrong, it's un-American, and the height of Bad Dad-ness!" And you know what? You're right. But so am I.

The reason I'm telling you not to ask your kids this question is simple: you already know the answer. That's right, the response you get from every single child, no matter what their age, is a monotone, monosyllabic, emotionless, uninformative, "Fine." That's it. Nothing else.

"How was school today, Heather?"

"Fine."

"Okay, um, great. So, Jason, how was school?"

"Fine."

"Glad to, ah, hear it. How about you, Dirk, Don, Debbie, and Danielle?"

"Fine."

"Fine."

"Fine."

"Fine."

Am I right or am I right? Now, being the Good Dad you are, you'll want to know everything that's going on in your children's lives. In fact, I'll go one step further and say that it's *imperative* you know what's going on in your children's lives. As their father, you need to know what they're doing, who they're doing it with, what teacher they like, what classes they don't like, who they walk to school with, what they do after school, and so on.

Simply asking them how school was or how their day went will not draw out the information you need. And if you interrogate them like some gestapo Dad, they'll clam up and never tell you anything. So here's what you do. Instead of asking them how school was, ask them, "What was your favorite part of the day?" This question gets them to think about their response, allowing them to open up to you, giving you more information and more insight into your child's life. Maybe even a little too much.

"So, Heather, what was your favorite part of the day?"

"Um, let's see … oh, I know, when Dylan smiled at me in the hall on the way to Algebra. Oh, Dad, he's so awesome! He's on the water polo team, and he plays guitar, and his older brother has a motorcycle and …"

See what I mean?

After you receive a satisfactory response, keep the conversation going by asking them, "Was there any part of your day that you didn't like?" Their response to this question could be quite benign, such as saying they hated the "mystery meat" they had for lunch in the school cafeteria. Or it could be surprisingly revealing. Sometimes a child's dislikes gives you a better window on their life than their likes. Either way, with either question, your children now have an opportunity to talk freely, and it gives you an opportunity to listen closely.

If, for some reason, you don't feel comfortable asking, "What was your favorite part of the day?" then don't ask it, you're not going to hurt my feelings. Come up with one of your own, just make sure it's open-ended enough to prevent your children from answering the obvious response of "Fine."

Got it?

Fine.

"So, Kelsey, what was your favorite part of the day?"

GOOD DAD

"So, Kelsey, how was school?"

BAD DAD

27

DESIGNATE ONE NIGHT A WEEK AS "FAMILY NIGHT"

Pick a night, any night. Now round up the kids, grab the Mrs., and—*voilá*—you've got yourself a Family Night.

Sort of.

Family Night is a wonderful way to spend quality time with your kids on a regular basis. The key phrase being "quality time." Sitting in the same room reading the newspaper while the kids watch cartoons doesn't qualify as quality time, let alone Family Night. So here's what you do: choose a night that's convenient for everybody. Decide on an activity that everyone agrees to. Do it every week, without fail. And, here's the key: do it *wholeheartedly*. In other words, be involved. Throw yourself into it 110 percent. Fill the night with fun, spirit, a true sense of *joie de vivre*. Then you've got yourself a Family Night.

Board games, card games, charades, heck, take 'em to a batting cage if that's what they want—whatever the family agrees on, do it. For you Good Dads out there with large families or huge gaps in the kid's ages, this poses more of a challenge. Use your imagination. Perhaps one week for the younger kids, one week for the older kids. C'mon, you can think of something—you're the *dad*.

Our kids are close in age so our Family Night—which happens to be Friday, the day both kids were born and the day we were married—has morphed into what we call "Popcorn Night." After eating a light dinner, I bring out this sprawling, oh-so-comfortable blanket and spread it on the floor in front of the TV. Meanwhile, my wife prepares a big salty, buttery batch of the best popcorn you've ever tasted. I don't know how she does it, but believe me, it's light years ahead of that microwave stuff.

(As an aside, it should be noted that the experts who study these matters suggest children under the age of 4 shouldn't eat popcorn because it's a choking hazard. So heed this warning.)

Okay, back to the subject at hand. We then let one of the kids select a movie of their choice from our vast collection of both videos and DVDs, pop it in, turn off the lights, and enjoy. In the winter I'll even light a fire in the fireplace. The glow from the fire makes the evening especially warm and cozy.

That's pretty much it. Nothing earth-shattering. Nothing to alert the media over. Just a simple, fun evening at home with the kids. But if you scratch below the veneer, it's much more than that. It's an incredibly bonding family moment that will bring back fond memories for years to come.

So whatever you do, do Family Night. It's good for the kids. It's good for the parents. It's good for the soul.

It's what Good Dads do.

"Whose turn is it to pick a movie?"

"I'll be out in the garage if you need me. And bring me a bowl of popcorn when you get a chance."

GOOD DAD

BAD DAD

28

WASH YOUR HANDS FREQUENTLY, ESPECIALLY DURING COLD AND FLU SEASON

Ah-CHOO!

Sorry, as I write this I'm suffering from a terrible cold. No one in my family is sick. No one at work is sick. None of my friends are sick. I have no idea how I caught this bug. But I do know how I could have prevented it. By washing my hands more.

Did you know that proper hand hygiene has been shown to *significantly* reduce the spread of the common cold and flu? And that it can eliminate nearly 50 percent of all cases of food-borne illness? To quote the U.S. Centers for Disease Control (CDC), "Hand washing is the single most important means of preventing the spread of infection." That's straight from the horse's mouth, guys.

The simple act of hand washing to prevent colds, the flu, even food-borne ill-nesses, is such a simple and fundamental solution it sounds almost crazy. But when you think about it, it makes total sense. What does a surgeon do right before he operates? Washes his hands. See? If it works in the operating room, why not in a public restroom?

When you touch a door handle, a gasoline pump, an escalator handrail, even a hotel remote, you have no idea who touched it last. Or where their hands have been. However, you do know where *your* hands have been. So if you've come into contact with anything that Joe Six-Pack can also get his grubby little mitts on, you need to wash yours. Frequently. And not just with water, either. Use soap. Regular soap. Not those antibacterial ones, which actually may do more harm than good. In fact, a large portion of the scientific community fears that widespread use of antibacterial soaps could lead to a strain of resistant bacteria or "super bugs." Besides, to kill bacteria, the soap has to remain on your hands for like 2 minutes.

Nowhere near a sink or running water? Keep a small bottle of those waterless, alcohol-based sanitizers at hand. These sanitizers kill 99.99 percent of the most common germs and they work in seconds.

So much data has been collected supporting good hand hygiene that certain states have developed instruction kits for use in schools and daycare centers on how to control outbreaks of colds, the flu, and other illnesses, and how to help teach the importance of proper hand washing.

By the way, Mom was right. Money is disgustingly dirty. According to a recent report, as many as 178,000 different types of bacteria can tag along on paper money—9,500 different strains of E. coli alone, not to mention fecal matter, which hides in all the nooks and crannies. During cold and flu season especially, wash your hands after every transaction. Oh, and wash your hands before putting in your contacts, too. Your eyes are like the portal to illness hell.

So wash your hands. A lot. Because when you can drastically cut your chances of getting sick by doing something this simple, that's nothing to sneeze at.

"Be right there. Let me wash my hands first."

"Ah ... ah ... AH-CHOO!"

GOOD DAD

BAD DAD

29

ENCOURAGE YOUR CHILDREN TO LEARN A FOREIGN LANGUAGE

Have you heard this joke before?

"What do you call a person who knows several languages?"

"A polyglot."

"What do you call a person who knows only one language?"

"An American."

It's no laughing matter. English is the universal language, true, but there's nothing wrong—and everything right—with increasing your children's chances in life by having them learn another language.

When should they start? Excellent question, mi amigo. The younger the better. Elementary school? Definitely. Pre-K? Sure, why not? You'll find classes at all levels.

The Center for Applied Linguistics (CAL) has a very excellent and enlightening pamphlet called "Why, How, and When Should My Child Learn a Second Language." The following information, which can be found on their website, sheds some light on the importance of learning a foreign language …

> *In addition to developing a lifelong ability to communicate with more people, children may derive other benefits from early language instruction, including improved overall school performance and superior problem-solving skills. Knowing a second language ultimately provides a competitive advantage in the workforce by opening up additional job opportunities. Students of foreign languages score statistically higher on standardized tests conducted in English. In its 1992 report, College Bound Seniors: The 1992 Profile of SAT and Achievement Test Takers, the College Entrance Examination Board reported that students who averaged 4 or more years of foreign language study scored higher on the verbal section of the Scholastic Aptitude Test (SAT) than those who had studied 4 or more years in any other subject area. In addition, the average mathematics score for individuals who had taken 4 or more years of foreign language study was identical to the average score of those who had studied 4 years of mathematics. These findings are consistent with College Board profiles for previous years.*
>
> *Students of foreign languages have access to a greater number of career possibilities and develop a deeper understanding of their own and other cultures. Some evidence also suggests that children who receive second language instruction are more creative and better at solving complex problems. The benefits to society are many. Americans*

fluent in other languages enhance our economic competitiveness abroad, improve global communication, and maintain our political and security interests."

I couldn't have said it any better.

If you want more information, or to order your own copy of this highly informative pamphlet, log on to www.cal.org. C'mon, be *Uberdad*, have a little *tète á tète* with the *niños* about learning another language, okay? Okay.

Ciao.

"You can take either Spanish, French, German, or Italian."

GOOD DAD

"Let's have dinner out tonight. What do you feel like— Spanish, French, German, or Italian?"

BAD DAD

30

DO

HELP YOUR CHILDREN WITH THEIR BOOK REPORTS BY READING THE SAME BOOKS

A former coworker of mine, "Barry," was an absolute book nut. He'd read a book a week, sometimes more. Crime novels. Mysteries. Memoirs. You name it, Barry'd read it. He loved books so much that his lunchtime was spent outside, in a beach chair, eating a sandwich and reading a book. I'd drive by this park near work and, sure enough, there was Barry sitting under a tree—reading. The whole scene looked so serene, so peaceful, I envied him and his love for books.

One day I stepped into the elevator and there was Barry, book in hand, head down, reading. The book was *The Adventures of Tom Sawyer*. I made a joke about how most guys read in the john, not the elevator. That's when he said he needed to finish the book before he got home that evening because his family was going to discuss it. "Damn," I thought, "this guy loves books so much he's getting his whole family involved." He explained further that his daughter was reading it for school, and that he was reading it to help her out.

FATHER FIGURE

Number of fathers who are part of married-couple families with their own children under the age of 18: 26.4 million

Apparently, a while back, his daughter had a book report due but labored with the book itself. Her grade, unfortunately, reflected her struggles. That's when Barry decided to read the next book with her. Wise decision, because his involvement helped tremendously. Not only was he able to shed some light on the parts of the book she didn't understand, but they shared some quality father-daughter time as well.

Barry has helped his daughter with every book report since, simply by reading the same book. The rest of the family is now involved, too. Kind of like a mini book club. He says it's really nice getting the whole family together to discuss *The Adventures of Tom Sawyer* or *Fahrenheit 451* instead of watching TV.

I couldn't agree more.

Hey, Barry, if you're reading this (and you should be, you read everything else on the planet), thanks for the Good Dad tip. I owe you one.

"Terrific, now let's discuss Chapter 6."

"Where's my TV Guide?"

GOOD DAD

BAD DAD

31

DON'T

ALLOW YOUR CHILDREN TO DO ANYTHING PERMANENT TO THEIR BODIES

Piercing. Scarification. Implants. Branding. Yes, even tattoos, all fall under the euphemistic umbrella called "body modification."

You're probably years away from having to worry about this, but I'm just warning you—just planting the seed for the future—not to let your kids fall prey to this pop culture vulture. It might be cool to have a full sleeve* when you're 19, but it's a whole different story when you're 40. Or 30. Or even 25, when these walking wall murals are looking for their first job in the corporate world. Let's put it this way: say a prospective employer has a job opening and two qualified candidates are both vying for the position. Both graduated from good schools, with good grades, have impeccable credentials and unblemished records. However one candidate looks "normal," while the other candidate—who just happens to be your son or daughter—has skulls, dragons, and half-naked hotties up and down his or her arm. Guess which one is going to get hired?

Now, not every one has indelible ink splashed across an entire limb. There are a lot of people with small, discreet tattoos. To me, these are almost acceptable. I say almost because they're still permanent. Hey, people change their minds all the time, and it's kind of hard to change something that's permanent. Like they say, a tattoo is permanent proof of temporary insanity. I'm guessing there's going to be a whole lot of regret in the later years when it comes to tattoos, even the subtle ones.

It amazes me that in such a short time, tattooing's reputation has gone from unsavory to mainstream. A recent poll states that 36 percent of Americans age 25 to 29 have at least one tattoo. And it's estimated that there are more than 15,000 tattoo parlors across this great land of ours. I'm astounded that so many people have a piece of art on their body that they would never hang over their sofa. When these kids are older and attending PTA meetings and parent-teacher conferences—not to mention high-level board meetings (if they get that far)— they're going to kick themselves.

Let's leave corporate America for a second and explore other areas of employment or service. Law enforcement and branches of the military, for example, are tightening rules for hiring employees in response to the increased popularity of permanent body art. The Coast Guard will now turn away any applicant whose

---

*A full sleeve is a tattoo or tattoos that cover an entire arm from shoulder to wrist.

tattoos cover more than 25 percent of an exposed limb. Even the Army has a long-standing rule that prohibits tattoos that show when the soldier is in uniform. The Navy, too.

Speaking of the Navy, my brother-in-law got his name tattooed on his bicep when he was younger. A simple tattoo by today's standards; four letters, cursive type, blue ink. He's now in his 60s and that thing has drifted down almost to his elbow, and it's an unreadable splotch.

Okay, enough about tattoos. Some body modification techniques are so extreme it's downright creepy. Have you ever seen anyone with a split tongue? Good Lord, it's so damn weird. The scarification and branding thing, too—I just don't get. Pierced ears? Okay, the holes can close up. But then you see kids with those huge, Lincoln-log things shoved through a gigantic hole in their earlobe, and when they take them out all that's left is this huge gaping hole and a dangling piece of loopy flesh. Again, who's going to hire these kids? It's not all about getting a job, but that's a big part of it.

So remember, as the Good Dad, tell your kids these four simple rules:

1. Ink is for paper, not skin.

2. Scarring is to be avoided, not self-inflicted.

3. Piercings, if they are to occur at all, shall remain the domain of the earlobe and shall be no larger than a pinprick. (For daughters, a pierced belly button may be acceptable, it's your call. If you've got a son who wants one, well …)

4. If any of these rules are violated, you're going to kick some serious butt.

"Wise decision to hold off on the ink. You're better off in the long run."

GOOD DAD

"An eagle across your entire chest? Honey, I'm so proud of you."

BAD DAD

32

DO

KEEP THE KIDS OCCUPIED ON FAMILY VACATIONS WITH THESE TRAVEL TIPS

"Are we there yet?"

"I have to go to the bathroom."

"I'm bored."

Sound familiar? If you've ever taken a trip with the entire family, I'm sure your little darlings have uttered these precious pearls somewhere along the way. Either at 35,000 feet or, say, right outside of Albuquerque. If you want to minimize the whining and complaining—and what Good Dad doesn't?—follow a few simple rules, or what I call Trip Tips. Take a look, then take your family on a nice long vacation and don't worry about a thing.

Trip Tip #1: Don't Mess with Dad. Kids are mess magnets. Wherever they go, especially in enclosed environs, a sticky, gooey mess is sure to follow. So be prepared with these superpower items:

- **Paper towels**—Bring several rolls to sop up anything your child can spill, drop, dribble, scatter, splash, or squirt on themselves—or on your butter-soft leather upholstery.

- **Plastic bags**—When the bag person at your local supermarket asks, "paper or plastic?" respond with the latter. These plastic bags are extremely handy for two things: 1) car trash, and, 2) if someone in the back seat decides to toss their animal cookies. Yes, car sickness, the scourge of the Good Dad. (It took us months to get regurgitated-Goldfish smell out of our car. Oh, if we only would have given our child a plastic bag to "toss" in.)

- **Large plastic bottle**—Just in case someone has to go #1 and there's no bathroom. Boys are a little easier with this one than girls. Their aim is better, and if there are trees around, bingo, instant bathroom.

- **Pull-ups**—Depending on the age of your children, have them wear pull-ups, even if they don't want to. They're easier to work with in case they have an accident.

- **Dramamine**—Reread second bullet point.

Trip Tip #2: Be prepared for a snack attack. It's no fun waiting to board a plane with a brood of bored kids. Trying to control the rioting masses on the second leg of a 7-hour road trip is no picnic, either. A quick fix? Snacks. Lots of 'em.

Breaks up the monotony and keeps the kids occupied. More importantly, keeps their mouths occupied. Nothing too messy, though, even if it's their favorite. Some snacks to consider are potato chips, pretzels, those gummy fruit-snack things, and some real honest-to-goodness fruits and vegetables. They'll also need something to wash all this down with, so bring drinks. Small bottles of water or sippy cups filled with their favorite beverage.

Trip Tip #3: Stay ahead of the game with games, toys, and gadgets. Part of being a kid is having fun. Traveling doesn't score very high on their fun-meter, but it can, if you bring along lots of stuff for them to do in the form of games, toys, and electronic gadgetry.

You've got the tried and true: paper, colors, pencils, cards, stickers, puzzles, and books. (Books, unfortunately, aren't recommended for children with touchy stomachs. Reading aggravates motion sickness.) A great idea is to give each child their own play area, such as a tray with sides on it. That way, pencils and crayons and such won't roll off. I know one dad who gives his daughter a cookie sheet to place on her lap as a tray.

As an added bonus, when each child has his or her own personal play space, there's no fighting over who gets what next. Don't get me wrong—there will still be fighting, just not over that.

Another idea is to get small, travel-size versions of checkers, chess, and other popular board games. Or get a handful of new toys from a discount retailer or dollar store and spring it on the little munchkins midway through the trip. They'll be thrilled. Hey, new toys are new toys, no matter how much they cost.

And don't forget all those road trip games that have been around for years. I Spy With My Little Eye, the License Plate Game, and 20 Questions. Or be the Good Dad and make up a game. How 'bout a spelling game? Or Guess How Many More Miles to the Next Fast Food Joint?

Gadgetry wise, if your kids are old enough, a GameBoy-type device is terrific. The individual games are pricey, but the kids enjoy playing them. But the *pièce de résistance* of the electronic crowd is a portable DVD player. We got one and, I'm telling you, it was a godsend. Worth twice the price if you ask me. If you have one in your vehicle, you know what I'm talking about. If you don't, get one. You'll thank me later.

In marriage, you're happy when your spouse is happy. As the Good Dad, you're happy when your kids are happy. So put these games and activities to good use. Down the road, you'll be glad you did.

"Road trip!"   *"What trip?"*

GOOD DAD   **BAD DAD**

33

DON'T

READ THIS CHAPTER

You know what I want you to do instead? Something with your kids.

Play a board game. Watch a DVD. Play catch. Take them to a park. Go on a bike ride. Or simply share a bowl of ice cream. It'll make you feel good. And it'll make them feel great.

Another thing. Whatever you decide to do with them, don't spend any money. Just spend time. Ultimately, time is what your kids really want from you, not what's in your wallet. Until they're teenagers anyway.

So what are you waiting for, Christmas? Stop reading and go already.

"He's right! Hey, Ryan, Mia, want to go to the park?"

"I don't get it. He said not to read this chapter, but I just read the whole thing. Maybe I better read it again, just in case I missed something."

GOOD DAD   **BAD DAD**

34

DIAPER
DUTY

Or should I say, diaper *doodie?* Because when your little bundle of joy arrives, that's what you'll smell for a long, long, *long* time. Doodie.

I know, I know, doodie is a wussy word, but this book is rated G, for all audiences. Believe me, the only grown man who would ever actually use the word "doodie" in conversation is Michael Jackson, so feel free to substitute the more common four-letter term.

Anyway, like they say, doodie happens. And you are going to be astounded at how *often* it happens. You'll be standing over the changing table, plugging your nose with one hand and wiping the cutest little tush with the other, wondering if your adorable little love muffin is normal. Or even human.

Along with a stench that could knock over a moose, questions will swirl around your brain, such as, "How can such a little person produce so *much?*" "Why does it smell so bad?" And of course, the inevitable, "What am I supposed to do with it?"

Okay, first things first. Changing diapers is a dirty job but someone's got to do it. And that someone is you, because that's what Good Dads do. Oh sure, your wife will probably do most of the work, but you need to pitch in, too. Not just to help her out. But to help you bond with your child.

That's right, every time you pick up your little angel and place him or her on the changing table, you make a connection. They look at you, you look at them. They study you, you study them. You notice little things about them that you never saw before. A freckle here, a dimple there. They smile, they coo, they gurgle. It's really quite adorable, an experience to savor, not dread. Before you know it, that tiny little person will be too big for the changing table, too big for diapers, too big for hugs. Too big for dad.

I worked with one woman who was pregnant with her second child. We got to talking and she let it slip that, with their first child, her husband never changed a diaper. Never. I was floored. I thought, "That lucky bastard." But the more I thought about it, the more I thought, "That poor bastard." He missed out on many, many wonderful, magical bonding experiences with his firstborn—experiences he'll never, ever get back.

Don't be that guy. Be the Good Dad. You won't regret it.

On a more practical note, you've got a decision to make: cloth versus disposable. Cloth diapers usually involve a diaper service. They come to your house, drop off a fresh load, and take back the dirty ones. With disposable diapers, you dispose of them yourself.

There are strong arguments for both. Some people claim cloth diapers are better for the environment because they're recycled. Others say disposable diapers are better because of all the detergent and water that's used to clean the cloth kind. Hey, it's a toss up. We used disposable; it just worked out better for us.

If you go the disposable route, I highly recommend a device called the Diaper Genie®. Basically it's a plastic diaper-disposal unit—kind of like a small trash can lined with a plastic bag. Put the dirty diapers in, twist the ring to close the bag, and close the locking lid, sealing in the smell. When it's full you simply take out the plastic liner, tie it shut, and dump it in the garbage. Easy. We used ours so often we had to replace it several times. Believe me, you'll use it. A lot. How often? Let me give you a little eye-opener, newbie.

My first taste of diapers—sorry, let me rephrase that—my first *experience* with diapers and what exactly is involved with them, was when my wife was pregnant with our firstborn and we took a Lamaze class through our local hospital. That's where I learned all about childbirth and newborns and parenthood. Some things were fascinating, others were better left unsaid. (Episiotomy, anyone?) But the instructor was great. She was friendly, patient, and informative.

However, one tiny little tidbit of info that she just happened to mention— almost as a throwaway, really—staggered me like I was hit in the head with a rock. *A newborn goes through 60 to 80 diapers a week.* "A week!" I thought. "No way!"

Yes way. Forewarned is forearmed. Sixty to eighty a week. But don't worry, after awhile you'll be so adept at changing diapers you could do it in your sleep. And at 3 in the morning, that's exactly what it's going to feel like.

By the way, if you just *have* to share the latest story about your child's latest bowel movement or pee episode because it's just too darn cute—don't. Other people really don't care. Honestly. Grandparents, maybe. Friends and coworkers? Not a chance, especially if they don't have kids themselves. So keep these stories to yourself. Trust me.

Oh, I almost forgot. For you dads out there with baby boys, I've got a tip for you: watch out for the unexpected "golden fountain." There you are, reaching for a diaper or cleaning a certain body part when—look out!—a stream of warm pee shoots out in all directions like a high-pressure garden hose. It splashes the walls, it drenches your clothes.

Well, after several good dousings, I finally got wise and figured out the perfect way to prevent this pee party; simply take out a new diaper and, after taking off the old one, gently place it over his young manhood. That way, if he does cut loose, the fresh diaper will absorb it. Genius.

Bottom line (pun intended), there are four good reasons to pull diaper doodie, er, duty. The two main reasons are, of course, #1 and #2. The third? Helping your spouse. And fourth is the bonding aspect.

See? No matter what, when it comes to changing diapers, you always come out smelling like, well, I was going to say roses, but Desitin is more accurate.

"I'll change this one, Honeybunch. You just sit and rest."

"Honey, little Colton just let off another stink bomb. Honey? Honey?"

GOOD DAD

BAD DAD

35

DO

FOLLOW A STRICT BEDTIME REGIMEN

Bedtime can be a wonderful, tender, loving, and precious time for you and your kids. Reading stories. Singing lullabies. Rocking them to sleep. Tucking them in. Kissing them goodnight. It's all so heartwarming … *sniff, sniff* … it's enough to bring a tear to a glass eye.

But beware.

Bedtime can be a troublesome, taxing, exhausting, and frantic experience if you don't implement and follow a strict code of correct conduct. Believe me, I know what I'm talking about, because I am *sooooo* guilty of not adhering to protocol. Yes, I was the Bad Dad, and on several occasions my wife wanted to throttle me. So pay attention, unless you enjoy wearing a neck brace.

To prevent rock-a-bye-baby from turning into rock-around-the clock, the most important rule to remember is this: create a bedtime regimen and *stick to it*.

Don't veer, stray, digress, divert, or deviate from this regimen one iota. If you do, that's it. A change in procedure throws everything off and makes it that much harder to get the little munchkins back on track. Children like routine. Makes them feel comfortable and secure. So set the course, then set sail.

FATHER FIGURE

Number of single fathers in the United States: 2.3 million

Rule number two: keep things calm before bed. This was my fall from daddy grace. I enjoyed playing with my two kids so much I didn't know when to stop. I'd wrestle with them, give them shoulder rides, tickle them, you name it, I did it. It was fun! And they thought it was a blast. Laughing, giggling, playing, having the time of their lives with dear ol' dad.

Then when bedtime rolled around, they were so stimulated it was an absolute nightmare trying to get them to sleep. They'd get out of their beds, they'd play with toys, they'd ask for water—*anything* but sleep. So for the sake of household harmony, don't get wild with your kids before bed. Understand, Stan?

Now that we got that straight, here's a suggestion that's slightly off topic but still worth mentioning. At some point your kids will transition from a crib to a "big girl" or "big boy" bed. This is a major step—it makes them feel all grown up.

But because cribs have sides and beds don't, you have to be careful they don't roll out and do a face plant on your newly polished hardwood floors. Our solution to this parent predicament? We placed the mattress and box spring directly on the floor—not on the bed frame—significantly reducing the drop from bed to floor.

For extra padding we even piled a couple of big stuffed dogs next to the bed, making these canine cushions almost flush with the mattress. Did this technique work? Like a magic amulet.

If you prefer, you can always get those attachable side rails for protection. Or splurge and get a "theme" toddler bed—you know, a fairy princess throne or big plastic fire truck, whatever your child's interest is at the time. One thing to keep in mind: if you're strapped for cash these beds can be pricey, and children usually outgrow them pretty quickly.

Another advantage to putting the mattress and box spring directly on the floor? Nothing spooky can hide underneath. Yep, you have to think about these things, because kids certainly do.

When I was young, I was afraid to dangle a limb over the side of my bed for fear that some hideous, child-eating monster was hiding under there. All it needed to be lured from its dark lair was a whiff of my tender, young flesh and—chomp!— I'd be toast. If my mom had only placed the mattress and box spring on the floor I wouldn't have suffered such trauma.

Speaking of things that go bump in the night, make sure all closet doors are closed, too. A sliver of darkness coming from the closet can send a child's imagination into overdrive and scare the bejesus out of the little tyke.

I used to go the extra step and poke my head in the closet, look around and say, "Nope, no monsters in here," then close the door. That extra bit of drama worked well.

Of course, kids are kids, and no matter what you do, they're going to be afraid of something come bedtime. For some reason Zach, our oldest, was afraid of lions. We tried reasoning with him, but because he was only 3, the fact that lions live in Africa did nothing to assuage his fears. So what I did was make a "Lion Stick."

I got a discarded paper towel roll, wrote LION STICK on it in big black letters and told him that the stick was magic and that it would keep lions away. And if a lion did happen to come into his room, all he had to do was bonk him on the nose with the stick and he'd run away and never come back. Problem solved.

Here's a tip I got from a coworker that's insanely ingenious. If your kids are afraid of, say, monsters, get a small plastic spray bottle and fill it with water. Write MONSTER SPRAY on the side, spritz it all around their room like mosquito repellent, and tell them the mist will keep the monsters away. I'm telling you, you pull this trick out some night and your wife will think you're some sort of daddy savant.

One last point and I'll get out of your rapidly receding hair. If your kids have a bad dream, let them know it's okay to come into your bed. Some parents will disagree with me on this; they feel it could turn into a habit that's hard to break. What can I say, I disagree with their disagreement. We never experienced a problem.

To tell you the truth, we enjoyed sleeping with them as much as they enjoyed sleeping with us. So go ahead, give your precious little angels an open invitation to climb in. It's not like you're having all that much sex anyway.

In summation, good kids need to follow rules. Good Dads need to follow rules too, especially when it comes to bedtime. So remember to implement and follow a strict bedtime regimen. Your kids will sleep better. And so will you.

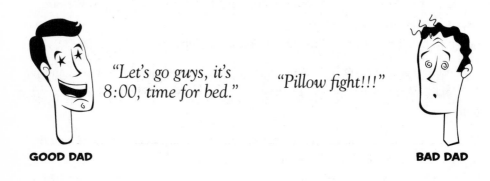

"Let's go guys, it's 8:00, time for bed."   *"Pillow fight!!!"*

GOOD DAD   **BAD DAD**

36

DO

POST ALL EMERGENCY PHONE NUMBERS IN AN EASY-TO-FIND PLACE

Code Blue! Code Blue!

Looks like we have an emergency on our hands, guys. It seems there are a lot of dads out there who don't have a readily available list of numbers to call in case of an emergency. Or if they do, they're not sure where it is. Or they think the only number they need to know is 911.

Are you one of these dads? Then it's time for a little crisis management.

Yes, 911 is still the Big Kahuna, the Grand Poobah, the Mother of all emergency phone numbers, but it's not the only one. There are a number of other numbers you need to keep handy, too, just to be on the safe side.

For example, it's Saturday night and you're trying out a new baby-sitter, the bright, responsible 14-year-old girl who just moved in down the street. Would she know how to contact your pediatrician at 10:37 P.M. if one of your kids suddenly got a fever that spiked to 104.8—and your cell phone, unbeknownst to you, had gone dead? Yeah, see, now you know what I'm talking about.

By the way, do *you* know how to contact your pediatrician without asking your wife for the number? (If this were a court of law you'd plead the 5th, wouldn't you?)

Next question. Do you know what numbers to include on your emergency list? And should you limit the list to just numbers? The following should help; it's the information my wife and I put together for ourselves. And, of course, for any poor soul brave enough to actually babysit our two boys, Cain and Abel, er, I mean Zachary and Alex.

- 911 (natch)

- Cell phone numbers (both yours and your wife's)

- Police department

- Poison Control

- Pediatrician's name and phone number

- Any allergies/medical conditions of your children

- A close relative's name and number (I'll explain later)

- Insurance company name and Group ID number

A couple things I'd like to mention at this point. First, you're probably wondering why I put 911 on the list. I mean, it should be so ingrained in your brain there's no need to jot it down, right? *Au contraire.* Yes, there is a need, and I explain it later in the chapter, so keep reading.

Second, regarding the "close relative's name and number," I included this on the list because my wife and I thought it was wise to give a close relative written consent to authorize any medical attention for our children in our absence. A baby-sitter can't—and isn't expected to—make a decision regarding medical procedures. We figured, in this day and age, you can't be too cautious when it comes to medical insurance and liability.

Of course, the above list is just an example of what to include. If I missed a specific number or category you feel is important, then by all means pencil it in.

In terms of where to put the list, don't shove it in a junk drawer where you have to claw your way through loose change, empty tape dispensers, old business cards, new telephone books, broken toy parts, rubber bands, paper clips, rulers, dried-up pens, and the mini solar-powered calculator you got from your bank last year. Keep it handy, Jim Dandy. Tape it on a wall near the phone. Better yet, tape it on a wall near *every* phone. Accidents aren't confined to just one area of the house, you know.

Another thing you might do is get several of those dry-erase, magic marker-type boards and place them in various locations around your house. These things make it a snap to add or change numbers, such as the phone number of the restaurant or friend's house where you'll be that particular night.

Okay, let's shake things up a bit. Let's say you and the little woman are out on the town and the babysitter slips on an errant toy, falls, hits her head on the corner end table, and is knocked unconscious.

Or you're at home eating a ham sandwich, you bite off more than you can chew, start choking, can't breathe, and Dr. Henry Heimlich is nowhere to be found.

Or, Heaven forbid, Grandma's watching the kids and keels over right there in the foyer. It could happen. Now what? The kids are fine, but the caretaker's down for the count. And the clock's ticking. That's why it's imperative to teach your kids how to dial 911.

Let them practice dialing it over and over again until they get it down. Do it on a toy phone, or unplug a real phone and teach them that way. Heck, make up a rhyme about it, or a song, so they remember it more easily.

Speaking of remembering, remember me telling you to write 911 on the emergency list? This is the reason—to serve as a reminder for your kids, not you. This small gesture just might save a life.

On a lighter note, here's a suggestion that doesn't pertain to an emergency situation, but it could help prevent a toddler meltdown. Tape step-by-step video/DVD player instructions directly on the TV remote for the babysitter.

Nowadays most every household has more than one remote, and it can get complicated and frustrating for someone who isn't familiar with your setup. And let me tell you, anytime you've got a brood of video-hungry kids jonesing for their favorite movie, things get ugly. Fast.

Let's review, shall we? Yes, 911 is still the Big Daddy of all emergency numbers. However, to be the Good Dad, you need to make a written list with other pertinent information and numbers as well, and post it in an easy-to-find place.

And do it now.

Before your wife declares a state of medical emergency on your slow-moving butt.

"There, a complete list of emergency numbers posted by every phone."

GOOD DAD

"Hey, here's that neat solar calculator I lost last tax season! And 27 cents! Sweet. Now ... what was I looking for?"

BAD DAD

37

DON'T
MAKE CHORES
SEEM LIKE A CHORE

Has your wife handed you your "Honeydew List" for the weekend yet? You know, "Honey, do this; Honey, do that." No? Then run, man, run!

But if the answer's yes, take off your track shoes, put on a smile, and don't grumble. Especially in front of your kids. Because if you gripe, grumble, and belly-ache about doing your household chores, how can you expect your kids to do theirs without griping, grumbling, and bellyaching?

For many things in fatherhood, example is the best teacher. Your kids look up to you and emulate you even when you think they're not paying attention. Their little eyes are always watching. Their little ears are always listening. Their little brains are always processing. So make sure they process the appropriate behavior and attitude when it comes to doing chores.

Which raises a good question: at what age should kids start doing chores? According to my sources, age 5 seems to be the magic number. But every child is different. If you have a 5-year-old who isn't mature, then hold back. On the flip side, if you have a preschooler who loves to pitch in and is developed enough to help out, by all means, wind him or her up and let the tyke take off.

The point is, start them young. Teach them at an early age about responsibility, cooperation, and commitment and these values will carry them through life.

What chores are best to start with? Common sense prevails here. Are you going to give a 4-year-old an axe and have the tot split a cord of firewood? Of course not. The words to remember here are *age-appropriate chores*.

For the youngest of the bunch, don't make their chores too challenging. Keep them simple. For example, have them pick up their toys. Or have them take their dinner plate to the sink when they're done eating. Start out easy, and then keep adding things for them to do. By slowly increasing your child's responsibilities, they grow more confident with every step and become ready, willing, and able to tackle tougher tasks as they get older.

Spread their chores throughout the house, too, not just their own personal space such as their bedroom. Branching out teaches them that, as a family unit, "we're all in this together."

Whether you have sons, daughters, or both, try not to be gender-biased in assigning chores. Have your son wash the dishes; have your daughter mow the lawn (after she's properly trained, of course). A boy getting dishpan hands and a girl getting a little dirt under her nails is good for them; makes them more self-sufficient, perhaps even more empathetic to the opposite sex and the so-called societal roles we're meant to follow. Both good, solid real-world lessons.

Some kids take to chores like a fish does to water. Others are more like *oil* and water … never the twain shall meet. They'll kick and scream and moan and complain and whine and cry and do everything they can to get out of doing chores. Whatever type of child you have, and I pray it's the former, you need a reward system.

One system that works well is a chart listing all their chores. Every time your child completes his or her assignments successfully, they get a sticker. When the chart is filled—say, every week—they get a reward. A special treat perhaps, or maybe allowing them to stay up past their bedtime.

Another reward system? The common allowance. It's odd to me, but some parents feel that the reward for completing one's chores shouldn't be of a material or monetary nature. They feel getting "paid" to help out around the house sends the wrong message and that contributing to the household is something every family member does because that's the way it is.

I don't know, the jury's still out in my mind. When I was a kid, I got an allowance, and getting that money gave me a real sense of accomplishment. We give our kids an allowance and I haven't noticed any negative side effects from them receiving a little dinero. (Come to think of it, they've started charging me a nickel for every hug. I just figured it was a sign of entrepreneurship, not poor parenting.)

The greatest reward to give your kids, however, is a good ol' pat on the back. Praise them. Praise them often. And praise them consistently. To a 5-year-old, a smile and an approving nod from Dad is worth more than all the money in the world.

"Bring it on, hon."

"But honey, the game's on. I'm not going to clean the yard right now! I'm not, I'm not, I'm not!"

GOOD DAD   **BAD DAD**

38

BE INSTRUMENTAL IN CULTIVATING A POSITIVE SELF-IMAGE IN YOUR DAUGHTER

I remember, years ago, seeing a birth announcement where the front of the card read …

Our baby was born without a penis.

The inside revealed …

It's a girl!

Cute. Because when you first read it you think, "Born without a penis, what the …?" It intrigues you. It mystifies you. It gets your curiosity up. Then when you read the inside you slap yourself in the forehead with your palm and say, "Of course, a girl. Silly me."

You automatically think "boy" first, even though the obvious answer is "girl."

Which is a fitting analogy for the way society works.

Yes, it's a man's world. Has been since time immemorial. And if you, as the Good Dad, don't want to perpetuate the notion that women are "the weaker sex" and that men are dominant in many situations, you need to cultivate a positive self-image in your daughter and boost her self-esteem from the day she's born.

The women's movement has made great strides, but there's still a lot of work to be done. To this day, women in the workforce earn less than men, even in the same job. And I'm sure you've heard the term "glass ceiling." Not many women can break through this discriminatory barrier. So with all these obstacles facing your daughter, a male influence early on can be extremely beneficial.

This is where you come in.

As the first important man in your daughter's life, your actions and behavior will have a profound impact on her. What you say, what you do, how you treat her, and ultimately how you treat all the women in your life, will affect your daughter in many ways, and shape her view of what men are like and should be like.

In the early stages of your daughter's life, simply be attentive. Be there for her in any way you can. As she matures, tell her you believe in her, and instill in her that she can do anything she wants. She will become stronger, more confident.

She'll be more likely to do well in school. More likely to continue her education into college. And more likely to do well in subjects and fields of work that, historically, have been male-dominated—such as math and engineering.

What can a lack of self-esteem do to a young girl? It can lead to behavioral problems, feelings of insecurity, promiscuity, and the inability to deal with relationship problems.

But it doesn't have to be like this. As I said, being the first important man in your daughter's life provides you with a unique opportunity to make her feel good about herself—not just for her looks—but for her abilities and accomplishments. They say a woman will marry a man just like her father. If this is true, what kind of a man will your daughter marry? Yeah, let that nugget marinate in your brain for a while.

Here's a thought. Have you ever asked a buddy of yours if he's glad he's a guy and not a girl? I guarantee with 100 percent certainty he'll say, "Yeah!" And he will no doubt preface his answer with a four-letter expletive that starts with "f" for added emphasis.

When I'm out and about and have to relieve myself like the proverbial racehorse, and there isn't a restroom in sight, I do what any red-blooded American guy does in this predicament—I duck behind the nearest bush or building. The entire time I'm standing there—standing being the operative word—I think to myself, "Man, I'm glad I'm a guy."

When I get ready to go to a fancy restaurant in 2 minutes flat, and I notice it takes my wife *forever* to pick out the right outfit (do guys even have "outfits"?), put on her makeup, decide what jewelry to wear, what purse goes with her shoes, how she should wear her hair, and so on, and so on, I think to myself, "Man, I'm glad I'm a guy."

When I was in the delivery room with my wife, sitting beside her, holding her hand, comforting her, watching her go through the ordeal of childbirth, I really, really, *really* thought to myself, "Man, I'm glad I'm a guy."

In the years to come, if your daughter finds herself in a situation—professional or personal—with a member of the opposite sex, and she thinks to herself, "Man, I'm glad I'm a girl," then you know you have succeeded in being the Good Dad.

"You can do whatever you put your mind to, Sweetie—I know you can."

"Oh my God, my baby's born without a penis! What? Oh, right, it's a girl ... ahem ... I knew that."

GOOD DAD   **BAD DAD**

39

FEED YOUR KIDS A HIGH-PROTEIN BREAKFAST BEFORE A TEST

Want your kids to get good grades? Don't just feed them knowledge, feed them a good breakfast.

It's the damnedest thing, but apparently true. Studies have shown that feeding your kids a high-protein breakfast the morning of a big exam can actually increase their mental faculties and boost their performance, giving them an edge. Wild, huh? And so easy to pull off, too.

"Here you go, Brianna … a ham and cheese omelet, a side of bacon, a cup of yogurt, and a protein shake. Anything else I can get you?"

"Yeah, Dad, like, a barf bag."

Yeah, Dad, like, let's keep things in food pyramid-perspective here. There's no need to go out and slaughter a team of oxen and force-feed it to your budding prodigy. Ideally the breakfast should be a healthy mix of low-fat, high-protein foods balanced with complex carbohydrates. That way you energize the gray matter *and* turbo-charge the body for sustained stamina. A few foods to consider for your child's morning repast include:

- Scrambled eggs

- Egg-white omelet with spinach and 'shrooms (great with a touch of Tabasco)

- Hard-boiled eggs (yolk or no yolk)

- Whole-wheat toast

- Whole grain cereals

- Oatmeal

- Granola

- Low-fat milk

- Cheese

- Low-fat yogurt

- Low-fat yogurt parfait

- Ham

- Bacon

- Canadian bacon

- Peanut butter

- OJ

- Fresh fruit

- Fresh fruit smoothie with protein powder

- Toad in the Hole (a slice of wheat bread with a 2 to 3-inch diameter hole cut out of the middle; place in a frying pan with some butter, pour a raw scrambled egg in the hole, cook until egg is firm, flip over and continue cooking until done)

- Breakfast sandwich (scrambled eggs, bacon, and cheese on multigrain bread)

- Breakfast burrito (corn or flour tortilla, Canadian bacon, egg whites, black beans, string cheese, avocado, and salsa)

Mix and match these foods any way you like, or round out the list by adding your child's favorite items. It's by no means a complete menu, just a few suggestions from *moi*. But remember, balance is key.

If your child has allergies or special dietary needs, you obviously have to take these into consideration. Better yet, talk to your pediatrician or a nutritionist if you have any concerns. But generally speaking, serve your child a sensible breakfast that's loaded with nutritious protein and complex carbs and your little Einstein will be off and running like a Cray computer, neurons firing at full capacity. Reality check: will a good breakfast guarantee they'll ace the test? Not if they don't study.

Are you and your family breakfast skippers? Down a cup of Joe and out the door you go? You may want to rethink that. Breakfast is the most important meal of the day. It's fuel to burn, baby, fuel to burn. Don't quote me on this, but I believe it keeps your metabolism revved up too, so you burn more calories, helping you lose weight.

Want to hear my own personal breakfast story? Tough, you're going to anyway. I'm a cereal kind of guy. I don't go for the sticky-sweet sugary kind; I enjoy the healthy, shredded-wheat/shredded-bran types. Anyway, I'd usually start my day with the morning newspaper and a bowl of the good stuff. Around 10:30 A.M., I'd get hungry and need something to munch on, and by lunch I could feel myself losing steam.

Then I heard about adding protein to every meal to keep your body humming along like a well-oiled machine. So I began making batches of hard-boiled eggs and squirreling them away in the fridge.

I'm telling you, when I started eating two hard-boiled egg whites after my cereal I felt like a new man. I'd cruise all morning long, with more energy, and not have to snack. Honest. And no, I'm not hypoglycemic. Adding low-fat protein to my breakfast simply helped my body run more efficiently. This minor nutritional adjustment worked like a wonder drug for me, and could for you, too.

Now aren't you glad you stuck around for the story? (I bet you're grabbing the car keys right now to get a dozen eggs, aren't you? That's my boy.)

Can you equate Good Dads with good grades? If a well-balanced, protein-rich breakfast is on the menu, you just might.

"A bowl of oatmeal and an egg white omelet ... good luck on the test, son."

GOOD DAD

"Sorry, Tyler, we're out of eggs. Have some Sugar-Frosted Choco Belly-Bombs with me."

BAD DAD

40

DON'T

CRITICIZE YOUR WIFE'S PARENTING SKILLS

Do you like having testicles? Because if you criticize your wife's parenting skills, which in her mind translates into criticizing how good of a mother she is, she'll be more than happy to rip them out—through your throat.

■ FATHER FIGURE ■

Total cost of raising a child from birth to age 18: $269,520

Keep your boys intact. Keep your mouth shut.

"You're doing a great job, sweetie. Keep it up."

[High, squeaky voice] *"What I meant to say was, you're doing a great job, sweetie. Keep it up."*

GOOD DAD   **BAD DAD**

41

DO

LIMIT THE AMOUNT OF TV YOUR KIDS WATCH

Remember when they used to call TV the idiot box? The boob tube? There's good reason: watching too much TV is bad for you. Or should I say, bad for your kids. Because, according to several studies, watching too much TV can actually harm your children's ability to learn.

As a parent, I don't disagree. Have you ever watched your kids watching TV? They completely zone out. It's like they're lobotomized. I'm serious. They get this glazed look in their eyes and their jaws go slack. You try to talk to them but they have so many lapses in their synapses they don't even hear you. Now, I'm no child psychologist, but to me, a vegetative state is not exactly the best frame of mind to be in when it comes to learning.

What's worse than having your kids watch TV in the comfort of the family rec room? Having them watch TV in the comfort of their own bedroom. One recent study showed that children with TVs in their bedrooms, with no computer at home, scored lowest on math and language arts tests. Not just lower, but *lowest*. Those with no bedroom TV, but who have home computers, scored the highest. Astonishing.

Evidence like that is hard to dispute. However, excessive TV watching is just one tine on this pitchfork. The other culprit is content. Have you seen some of the shows on TV these days? Pretty graphic. Pretty violent. Pretty sexual. Not a pretty picture when you're trying to raise a family. It's well documented that kids exposed to violent images day in and day out get desensitized, which leads to an increase in violent behavior. Now studies are finding that repeated exposure to sexual imagery leads to more and more teenage promiscuity.

So what's a father to do? Curb what your kids watch and be vigilant about it. If you don't want them to watch a particular program, don't let them. It's that simple. Turn it off, change the channel, take away the remote—do *something*, for God's sake. Be proactive. You're the parent. They're the child. You make the rules, they don't. Period. Same holds true for movies, music, and video games. If you don't like it, they don't watch it, listen to it, or play it.

By the way, don't underestimate the power of advertising, either. Kids are bombarded with dozens and dozens of commercial messages every day for the sugariest (is that even a word?) cereals, the lamest toys, the trendiest clothes, and the unhealthiest fast foods. And they're going to want it all.

Daddy, I want that!

Please, daddy?! Please, please, please, please, please!? I promise I'll be good.

But daddy, it looks really, really, really, really, really, really, really, really, really, fun! Pleeeeeeaaaaaase?

Be strong. And don't cave in. Tell these future consumers how commercials—and television in general—distort the truth and make everything seem really cool, really delicious, and really fun when they're really not.

The influence of advertising became abundantly clear to me one morning when our youngest, who just turned 5, asked my wife and me at breakfast if he could have chocolate milk with his pancakes instead of regular milk. Because it was the day after Easter, and knowing how many chocolate rabbits, marshmallow eggs, jellybeans, and malted milk balls he consumed the day before, we denied his request. He looked up at us and said, with the straightest of faces, "But the man on TV said that chocolate milk is a great way to start your day."

Here was this wide-eyed, innocent child, with the sweetest little face and most angelic voice, reciting—word for word, mind you—a completely fabricated selling message from some talking head on TV! I almost coughed up a lung I laughed so hard. Oh, the power of television on young, impressionable minds.

In television's defense, a number of shows and children's programs are educational, engaging, and really, really funny. Some of these programs have been on the air for years. Some of them are new. There's nothing wrong with any of them, but if it comes to watching TV, reading a book, or playing outside, what would you choose for your kids? I thought so.

I hate to admit this, but TV does come in handy as an electronic babysitter. Let me explain; when our first born came along, my wife read something about not letting your child watch TV for the first 2 years of his or her life. Our naiveté got the best of us, so we tried it. We read lots of books and played age-appropriate games, along with an educational video or a TV show or two.

Then came our second child, right on the heels of the first. (They're only 20 months apart. Can you say, "oops"?) The second one watched more TV in his first year than the oldest did in two. Why? Because with two rambunctious boys so close in age, we needed a break, and if we didn't get a little respite from life's daily aggravations we would've spontaneously combusted. So we put them in front of the tube, that way we can finish the laundry, make dinner, do the dishes, or just get a little peace and quiet. Sometimes you must do what you must do, even if it goes against the rules. That's the reality of parenting.

On another note, people like statistics, so here's one for you: the average American family has 2.4 TVs in their household. (I'd like to know which family member gets stuck watching the .4 one.) I expect that number to trend up, quite frankly. I know a family that has a TV in their living room, one in each bedroom, one in the den, and one in the kitchen. You walk into their house, and it's like being in the electronics section of a department store.

Look, television is not evil. But if your kids want their MTV, simply parcel it out in small doses. Set reasonable limits, and make time for both active play and quiet reading.

This has been a message from the Emergency Good Dad System.

"That's enough TV, guys. Time for homework."

"That's enough homework, guys. Time for TV."

GOOD DAD

BAD DAD

42

DO

LEARN ABOUT MAKE-UP AND CLOTHING—IT'S *EXTREMELY* IMPORTANT TO YOUR DAUGHTER

To paraphrase Ray Bradbury, who borrowed from Shakespeare,

"By the pricking of my thumbs, Something tricky this way comes."

Tricky indeed, for you are about to embark on a journey few men dare to undertake. A journey that will transport you to a land so foreign that most males will find the terrain too difficult to navigate without assistance. A land strewn with so many pitfalls and landmines that one misstep by the foolhardy will result in apocalyptic catastrophe.

This place of which I speak? The Land of Tween, inhabited by daughters everywhere whose only thoughts are composed of hair and make-up and clothing and jewelry—*AND BOYS!*

[Hand slap across face]

Get a hold of yourself, man! Yes, it's scary and treacherous but, if you have a daughter—no matter how young—you must sail these uncharted waters at some point. So stand up straight, throw your shoulders back, and march forth like a man with bravery, courage, and mettle.

Or ... do what I did: ask your wife how to handle the situation.

Yeah, I wimped out. When I concluded that *Good Dad/Bad Dad* needed a chapter on this topic, I had no personal experience whatsoever. Sure, I watched it from the sidelines as my four older sisters were growing up, but seeing it through the eyes of a young boy is different than seeing it through the eyes of a loving father.

I wanted to be as accurate as I could and not give you any misleading information. That's when I had a brainstorm and decided to go to the oracle of all-things female: my wife, Maureen. She went through this situation with her dad and they both seemed to come out of it relatively unscathed. So I walked right up to her, grabbed her by the shoulders, looked her square in the eye, gave her my best Clint Eastwood squint, and said, "H-E-L-P!"

So here you go, guys, words of wisdom straight from the voice of experience. Take it away, Maureen ...

"To start, realize that young girls like to experiment with clothes and jewelry that make them look older. As their father, you might wince at this at first, but keep in mind this is their way of trying out grown-up roles, just as they do when they play with their dolls.

"It's just child's play, so try not to be too alarmed. However, it is appropriate to put some limits on it if you or your wife feel your daughter is going too far and becoming too sexy or sassy."

(You can tell a woman wrote the preceding paragraph. A guy would never use the word "sassy." Okay, let's continue.)

"When girls become preteens, or tweens, they naturally become more interested in wearing make-up. Having the latest brand-name clothes becomes very important, too.

"A large part of this is trying to fit in with the crowd. Their peers are becoming more important to them as they try out new roles and start forming their own identity. As with clothes and jewelry when they are younger, realize that this is all part of a developmental phase and is quite normal. Again, set limits if you feel it's going too far.

"Also during this time, remind your daughter—and keep reminding her—that although you realize her appearance is very important to her, her other attributes and accomplishments are just as important, if not more so."

(I devote an entire chapter to the subject of cultivating a positive self-image because I feel it's that important. Check out Chapter 38.)

"This may be a few years down the road for you, but when girls go to a dance, they will naturally want to wear more make-up than they do every day. Their daily make-up might include mascara and tinted lip-gloss. For a dance, they'll probably want to add blush and eye shadow.

"And steel yourself for the dresses they'll want to buy—they can be expensive, and maybe a little more revealing than you anticipated, but the dress a girl wears to a dance is all-important, so don't be too harsh in your judgment. Just look at this as a dress rehearsal for your daughter's eventual wedding, and get used to the sticker shock."

Terrific stuff. Thanks, Maureen. But, man-oh-man, tinted lip-gloss? Mascara? Blush? Eye shadow? Daily make-up versus dance make-up? Might as well be speaking Esperanto. But if you have daughters, these are words you need to know.

Face it, guys. Daddy's Little Girl will grow up someday. But that "someday" isn't here yet. So enjoy your daughter in all phases of childhood, and embrace her changes.

Me? I have two boys; I don't have to worry about this stuff at all.

Good luck, fellas.

"You look very nice, Jen. My little girl is growing up."

"What the …? Where's the circus? I've seen clowns wear less make-up!"

GOOD DAD

BAD DAD

43

DON'T
WORRY

As a parent, you're going to worry about your kids being ...

Too fat.
Too thin.
Too hot.
Too cold.
Too introverted.
Too extroverted.
Too short for their age.
Too tall for their age.
Not smart enough.
Not cool enough.
Not popular enough.
Not healthy enough.
Not good-looking enough.
Not funny enough.
An underachiever.
An overachiever.
A Type A personality.
A "no personality" personality.

You're going to worry whether ...

They have to wear glasses.
They have to get braces.
They have no drive.
They have no friends.
They get a pimple.
They get detention.
They need a tutor.
They need a speech therapist.
They're developing too early.
They're developing too late.
They're an only child.
They're a lonely child.
They're bed wetters.
They're not go-getters.

You're going to worry that they're not …

Eating enough vegetables.
Drinking enough milk.
Getting enough exercise.
Getting enough sleep.
Staying ahead of the curve.
Staying the course.

You're going to worry about …

Your kids and drugs.
Your kids and sex.
Your kids and smoking.
Your kids and drinking.
Your kids and their friends.
Your kids and their enemies.
Your kids and peer pressure.
Your kids and sexual predators.
Your kids and depression.
Your kids and their relationship with you.

You'll worry about …

Birth defects.
The birthing process.
The infant years.
The preschool years.
Grade school.
High school.
Graduate school.
Dropping out.
Online chatrooms.
Bullies.
High fevers.
Low grade-point averages.
Bicycle accidents.
Car accidents.
Broken bones.

Night terrors.

Growing pains.

Terrorist attacks.

Asthma attacks.

Safe sex.

Unsafe sex.

Teen angst.

Teen pregnancy.

Their future.

Their future spouses.

Peanut allergies.

Any allergies.

Mutating viruses.

Drug-resistant bacteria.

Diabetes.

Cancer.

AIDS.

And a zillion other things you can think of.

In other words, you're going to worry about *everything*. I'm here to tell you—don't. Easier said then done, I know, but worrying won't change the outcome, all it does is waste a lot of mental energy that could be put to better use. And when you stand back, take a deep breath, and put everything into perspective, 99.9 percent of the stuff you worry about will never happen. Or if it does, it won't be as bad as you thought.

Like the song says, "Don't worry, be happy!" Think good thoughts, not bad thoughts. Think Good Dad, not Bad Dad.

"Que sera sera."

"WHERE'S MY XANAX?!"

GOOD DAD   **BAD DAD**

44

DON'T

YELL OR
LOSE YOUR
TEMPER!!

There are two ways to communicate with your children:

1. Like this.
2. OR LIKE THIS!!!

Let's say you have a bad day at work. You come home in search of a little R & R but for some reason the kids are in a mood. You ask them to please pick up their clothes ... or turn off the TV ... or do their homework ... and they simply don't do it. They're just not listening.

So you ask them—for the second time, mind you—to *please* pick up their clothes, turn off the TV, or do their homework. Again, bupkus. Your patience is wearing thin and their inattentiveness is making you angry. Really, really angry. The fuse has been lit.

A brief moment passes—and now it's the third @#%* time you ask them. At this point, the only thing you're getting with your kids is more and more ticked off.

The fuse is getting shorter and shorter, until you just can't take it anymore, and then finally ...

KA-BOOM!

YOU ERUPT LIKE KRAKATOA! YOU'RE YELLING, YOU'RE RANTING, YOU'RE RAVING! YOUR KIDS ARE STUNNED INTO INACTION, MAYBE EVEN A LITTLE SCARED. AND YOU KEEP RIDING THEM AND RIDING THEM AND RIDING THEM AND YELLING AND SCREAMING AND CURSING! YOU TELL THEM IN NO UNCERTAIN TERMS THAT YOU ARE SO MAD YOU COULD SPIT NAILS AND THEY BETTER PICK UP THEIR CLOTHES—OR TURN OFF THE TV—OR DO THEIR HOMEWORK— RIGHT NOW! RIGHT THIS INSTANT! OR ELSE!

As you can see, it's not very pleasant being on the receiving end of someone's conniption, is it?

IS IT? ANSWER ME! WHAT IF YOUR BOSS COMMUNICATED TO YOU LIKE THIS? WOULD YOU BE MORE PRODUCTIVE? WOULD YOU TRY HARDER? I DON'T THINK SO. WHAT ABOUT YOUR SPOUSE? WOULD THAT STRENGTHEN YOUR RELATIONSHIP OR CHIP, CHIP, CHIP AWAY

AT THE VERY FOUNDATION OF YOUR LOVE FOR EACH OTHER UNTIL THERE'S NOTHING LEFT? HUH? HUH? SO WHY COMMUNICATE WITH YOUR KIDS LIKE THIS? LOOK AT ME WHEN I'M TALKING TO YOU!

Ah, much better to communicate this way, isn't it? Be clear. Be stern. But keep your anger in check. Take a few deep breaths, count to 10, and if you can muster up a little humor, try that too.

Oh, I can hear it now, "David to Earth, David to Earth, do you read me?" No, I'm not from another planet, and no, my name's not Pollyanna either, wise guy. I know kids can get the best of you, and sometimes you just can't help but fly off the handle. All I'm proposing is that you at least try to curb the yelling, and to temper your temper with a little levelheadedness.

OKAY?

Okay.

"Stevie, this is the last time I'm going to say this: please turn off the TV. Now."

GOOD DAD

"STEVIE, THIS IS THE LAST @#% TIME I'M GOING TO SAY THIS! TURN OFF THE @#%* TV! NOW!!!"*

BAD DAD

45

SUGGEST YOUR KIDS TAKE AT LEAST ONE DRAMA OR ACTING CLASS

What is the number one fear of most people? If you guessed glossophobia, you are correct, sir.

Glossophobia is so prevalent, in fact, it is believed to affect three-quarters of the population. It even surpasses the fear of death. Wow.

For you dads out there suffering from "dictionaryphobia," or if you don't feel like getting off your keister to look it up, glossophobia is the fear of public speaking. Okay, now where were we? Oh, yeah …

It's easy to understand why people are scared to speak in public. Having all eyes on you is unnerving to say the least. Palms sweat. Voices quaver. Stomachs turn. Minds go blank.

The thing is, speaking in front of people is crucial to adult success. So the best thing to do is to start working on it in childhood. That's right, nip it in the bud before the stage fright bug digs its insidious claws into your child's psyche and turns them into a quaking, shaking blob of Jell-O before every oral report, speech, or presentation they'll ever give. For the rest of their lives.

FATHER FIGURE

Most collect calls are made on Father's Day

That's why drama class needs to take center stage. Enrolling in a drama or acting class, or simply trying out for the school play, can definitely help ease the anxiety and panic one feels when talking in front of people. Why? Because the key to getting over one's fear of public speaking is confidence. And what builds confidence? Experience.

The more you do something, the better you get at it. The better you are, the more confident you are. The more confident you are, the more persuasive you are. The more persuasive you are … okay, you get the idea.

My boss is an excellent presenter. She gets up in front of a crowd without a lick of fear. She's energetic, she's demonstrative, she's confident. Guess what her major was in college? Drama. Is she an actress? No. Does she have the crowd eating out of her hand after every meeting? Yes.

That's how I want my kids to be. Heck, that's how *I* want to be. I mean, I can hold my own in a group, but I pale in comparison to her. Guess I should've majored in drama.

Here's a tip that might help your child: have them break routine, or do something out of the ordinary that no one in the audience is privy to. It worked for me.

When I was in college, I had to give a major presentation for my marketing class. It was for half my grade. I knew the material well, but I was still nervous because of the importance of the presentation and its impact on my GPA. For some reason—I don't even remember why—we had to dress up; suit, tie, the whole nine yards. Know what I did? Or I should say, know what I didn't do? I didn't wear socks. There I was, in my best suit, with a new tie, spit-shined black dress shoes—and no socks. No one knew but me, and for some strange reason it gave me confidence.

The lack of socks was like my own little secret, and this mischievous bit of knowledge helped me make light of the situation, which made me relax more. Needless to say I aced the presentation. Who knew?

Having your kids take an acting class won't turn your drama queen into the next It Girl, or your boy into America's newest leading man. However, the practice and experience can turn them into a better speaker, thus improving their communication skills and giving them the confidence that will help them in their chosen career.

It's like the old joke …

Tourist: "How do you get to Carnegie Hall?"

New Yorker: "Practice."

"I think it'd be good for you, Jess."

GOOD DAD

"Nah, you don't need a class—just picture your audience naked."

BAD DAD

46

SET ASIDE SOME "ME TIME" EVERY DAY

"You inconsiderate lout."

Hear that?

"Why you selfish ignoramus."

You must've heard that one.

"How dare you put yourself and your needs ahead of your kids?"

That one couldn't have been any clearer.

"And you call yourself a Good Dad."

Ouch. That last one might've hurt if I didn't feel so strongly about this subject, but I do, so it didn't.

What I'm getting at is this: there's a contingent of dads out there who aren't exactly in my corner on the topic of daily "me time." They feel it's an egotistical and self-centered approach to fatherhood and that any dad claiming to be 100 percent devoted to his children wouldn't take such a narcissistic stand.

This assemblage of dads agrees, of course, that doing something for yourself is justified every now and then, but every day? They say no. You know what I say? I say, hey, everybody's entitled to their own opinion, this personal belief isn't hurting anybody. Is it?

Allow me to explain with an example. You and the family are on your first vacation in years and you're winging it to Maui. You board the plane wearing a vintage Hawaiian shirt, flip flops, cargo shorts, and a very broad smile.

Your wife's looking sultry in her sky-blue, bird-of-paradise sarong, even though it is a tad tighter than it used to be. (BTW: Keep this last bit of knowledge to yourself unless you want to experience what its like getting sucked out of one of those little windows at 30,000 feet.)

Your kids are fairly young in age—if they're not, just play along—and they're all excited because it's their first trip to Hawaii. Heck, maybe it's their first time on a plane.

You settle in for the long flight just as the flight attendant begins her safety spiel, demonstratively pointing out the emergency exits, and so on. As the Good Dad, you make sure your kids are paying attention because this is very important information she's gesticulating about.

You listen intently as the flight attendant explains what would happen in the unlikely event the cabin loses air pressure. She demonstrates how the oxygen masks will drop from above, how you must pull on the elastic ties to activate the airflow, and how you place it over your nose and mouth and inhale deeply. And when you're all squared away with your own oxygen mask, you may then proceed to help those who need assistance with theirs. In other words, *your children.*

Wait a minute, you think to yourself. Did she just say what I think she said? Put the oxygen mask on yourself first and *then* help your children? That can't be right. I'm a good father, a devoted dad, and I'm going to always, always attend to my children's needs ahead of mine.

Aha! But the airlines, in this case anyway, know what they're talking about. By helping yourself and putting your basic needs first, *you* are *helping your children.* Because if you don't keep your wits about you, and something happens to you, no one's going to be around to help them.

No one.

This same airplane logic applies to fatherhood at home, too. It's the reason why I say that you, as a Good Dad, must set aside some time for yourself every day. Away from the kids. Away from the wife. Away from responsibility. So you can be at your best, to help your kids be their best.

There's a lot of pressure that comes with being a dad. And if you're not stressed, you're not paying attention. Work, bills, health issues, college funds, retirement funds, over-scheduling—you name it, it builds and builds. Day in and day out. But if you carve out some time for yourself on a daily basis, it allows you to let off some steam and decrease the pressure.

Think of it as giving yourself a timeout. Only it's not a punishment, it's more like a temporary, self-imposed exile from the United Republic of the Daily Grind. This little slice of "me time" will actually help you be a better dad because it recharges your batteries and helps you appreciate the time you spend with your kids that much more.

What can you do? Do what you want. Read a book. Ride a bike. Watch sports. Play sports. Listen to music. Play some music. Whatever it may be, do it. You're not being selfish, you're being smart.

Uh-oh—hear that? I think I created a monster with that last paragraph. Now it seems there are legions of dads out there whoopin' and hollerin' and jumpin' all around thinking they've got carte blanche to go out and play 18 holes of golf whenever they feel like it. Sorry, guys. You're just as misguided as the well-intentioned dads who disagreed with me in the first place.

You can't just go out and pleasure yourself, if you will, at the expense of your family. You set aside this special time alone to become a better father, not a deadbeat dad. I'm talking 30 minutes away from the kids to read the sports section, not a nightly jaunt to your local Hooters for wings and brews. If that's what you're thinking, then you, my friend, truly are an inconsiderate lout, a selfish ignoramus.

You know what my wife encouraged me to do? Get a "cave." You know, set aside a room in the house that serves exclusively as a respite, a retreat, a decompression chamber I could escape to and indulge myself in any troglodyte pursuit I felt like doing. (Yeah, she's a keeper.)

A close friend of mine has a "cave" in his house. It's a small side room filled with a profusion of personal belongings, such as his own computer, a high-end stereo, an electric guitar, a small amp, a library of books and magazines, a small swivel chair—and a secret stash of top-shelf, premium tequila. When he needs to get away, he cloisters himself in this architecturally challenged room and does what he does. He says it works wonders. (I have a feeling the tequila has a lot to do with it.)

What I really like about the whole cave idea is that you have your own private space to chill out in, but you're still at home, just in case something were to happen and your fatherly presence is needed. Now that's a Good Dad.

Still think that carving out a daily sliver of "me time" is selfish, narcissistic, and egotistical? Too bad. Because the ego has landed. And it's landed smack in the middle of Good Dad territory.

"Honey, if you need me I'll be in my cave."

"Sorry, babe, can't hear you, it's really loud in here. What? All right, all right, I'll be home right after this next pair of hoot—I mean, order of wings."

GOOD DAD

BAD DAD

47

DON'T

GET A FAMILY PET IF YOU CAN'T CARE FOR IT PROPERLY

When I was a kid, I asked my mom if I could have a pet chameleon. She hemmed and hawed. I begged and pleaded. She finally gave in, and I was the happiest kid on the street. She called the local pet store and they said they'd have it in a week.

That week seemed like a year; I couldn't *wait* to get my new chameleon. Finally, on the seventh day, I did not rest. We drove to the pet store the minute it opened, and I proudly walked in ready to claim my new best friend.

The "animal sales representative" said he'd have to go in the back to retrieve it. I heard what sounded like a scuffle coming from the backroom, like claws scratching on cardboard and objects falling to the floor, but thought nothing of it. The guy finally came back out, triumphant, grinning broadly and said, "Here you go, young man, he's all yours."

I can only imagine the look on my face. It must've been pure shock and horror. In this guy's arms was a 4-foot-long, lime green, prehistoric relic; a throwback to the age of reptiles. An ugly, scaly, frightening, true Creature from the Black Lagoon.

An iguana.

I could barely speak, I'd never seen anything like it before. After I picked my eyeballs off the floor and put them back into their sockets, I finally managed to eke out two words: "What's ... that?" He responded, "An iguana, the one you ordered."

Long story short. I wanted a chameleon, but inadvertently asked my mom for an iguana. (How I got those two creatures, and those two words mixed up, are beyond me. Hey, I was a kid, give me a break.) Needless to say, we didn't get Godzilla. We settled for a regular, run-of-the-mill chameleon. I was happy, and more than a little relieved.

It died 3 days later.

Two things all Good Dads need to learn from this. One, never let me take care of your pet chameleon. And two, get a pet that's appropriate and fitting for your family's lifestyle.

When it comes to pets, families are similar to individuals—they have distinct personalities. Some families are dog families, others are cat families. Then you've got your fish families, bird families, and guinea pig/gerbil/hamster/rat families. Even the Burmese Python families. (I saw one of these legless monsters swallow a whole baby rabbit in a pet store once. I couldn't eat for the rest of the day.) If you live in a rural area of the country you've got your pig, goat, cow, horse, and sheep families, too.

Whatever pet you and your family get, God love ya. Pets are more than just a welcome addition to a family, they *become* family. But they are also a commitment. A living, breathing, eating, feeling commitment you can't walk away from should you or your kids get bored.

This happens a lot around holidays, especially Easter. Kids see baby chicks, for example, or baby bunnies, and they want one. So being the, uh, "good" parent, you indulge them. Guess what happens to baby chicks and baby bunnies? They grow into chickens and rabbits. They're not so cute anymore and they require a lot of work. The kids grow tired of the animals and the parents grow tired of the maintenance. So these once-adorable animals get abandoned. Or they're "taken care of" in ways, I feel, are better left unsaid.

Here's the joyous part. Dogs and cats and other pets can bring an immeasurable amount of happiness and joy to your family. Studies have even shown that owning a pet can help with self-esteem and even lower blood pressure. Children can also learn about responsibility.

Is there a downside to owning pets? Hmmmm, well, yes and no. For instance, if your wife is preggers, and you already own a cat, don't let her clean the litter box. She could contract toxoplasmosis, a parasitic disease.

If you have reptiles, such as an iguana, you have to watch out for salmonella. And if you have a newborn in the house and you're thinking of getting a dog, you might rethink acquiring one of the more aggressive breeds such as a pit bull or rottweiler. You definitely want a kid-friendly breed.

Picking out a pet as a family is a good way to go. That way, everyone's in on the process, everyone has a sense of ownership, and everyone can assess the animal's personality (yes, animals have personalities) to see if it meshes with the family's. If a dog or cat is on your list, I recommend going to an animal shelter. Or you can go to your local pet store. Either way, you'll do fine.

Finding a pet is the fun part. Losing one is a different story. Yes, lose, as in dies. You're a man, an adult—I feel confident in your ability to handle the loss. I'm sure you've lost things before. Your virginity, for one. And quite possibly, your hair. But other than a tooth or an occasional sock, your kids haven't lost anything of worth, and losing a family pet can be traumatic.

Should this happen, don't tell them that Rex went to live on Grandma's farm. Tell the truth. Tell them it's okay to be sad and help them work through their grief. They're kids, they're resilient, they'll bounce back pretty well.

Know what my pet peeve is? People who procreate then procure a pet for their progeny that's inappropriate for their pet personality profile. Yep, a palpable presence of problems and pitfalls could be possible.

Whew.

However, if you think it through and conclude that the work and commitment are worth it, then by all means get a pet.

"A pet's a good idea, but let's look at it from all angles."

"Awesome, a Komodo Dragon!"

GOOD DAD

BAD DAD

48

DO

PITCH IN WHEN IT COMES TO FEEDING

"Slept like a baby!"

Oh, did you now? Then you must've been awfully uncomfortable, waking up every 2 hours. Hungry. Crying. With soiled undergarments. Because, truth be told, that's how newborns sleep.

If you have kids, you know what I'm talking about. If you're about to have your first, well, good luck, son, you'll need it. But what you really need is to help your wife any way you can. Remember, she's the one who recently pushed out a fully formed human being, approximately 8 pounds in weight and 20 inches in length of pure cartilage, sinew, and bone, through a portal only a few centimeters in diameter.

You try passing a grape through your schwanz and then you tell me if you need assistance caring for your newborn because, well, you know, you might be a tad sore.

Now that this thought is permanently etched into your memory banks, back to the topic at hand: pitching in after the baby arrives. Specifically, feeding.

Feeding is a nonstop, round-the-clock chore that must be performed no matter what time it is. Three in the afternoon or three in the morning—if that little person is hungry you must feed its need. But before reality upsets your circadian rhythm, you and your wife must make the decision: breastfeed or bottle-feed.

(Note: Here's where I talk about breasts, so please try to contain yourselves, gentlemen.)

My vote is for breastfeeding. There's no formula on Earth quite like the one ol' Mom Nature gives all new moms. Breastfed infants have fewer medical problems—such as ear infections, allergies, and diarrhea—than bottle-fed babies.

Sucking at the breast (down, boy) also promotes good jaw development because it's harder to get the milk out of a breast than a bottle. And breastfeeding might have psychological benefits due to the skin-on-skin contact between mother and baby.

If that's not enough, one aspect of breastfeeding that appeals to every hard-working new dad is that it saves you money. That's right, Midas. You don't have the expense of buying bottles and nipples and formula, which really adds up after awhile.

The icing on the proverbial cake? It's not your man boobs the baby's snacking on, it's your wife's breasts, and her breasts alone. Which is a comfort when it's 2:37 A.M. and you hear the unmistakable *wah-wah* of your newborn. You nudge your wife, tell her the baby's crying, and then drift back to slumberland. In other words, you're off the hook, baby. Right?

Not so fast, bub.

Your wife's exhausted, her nipples are sore and cracked, and she's seriously thinking of crowning you with the alarm clock unless you lend a hand. Here's where you pitch in. Store some bottles of expressed breast milk in the fridge and you take over the feeding. Tit for tat, if you will. This way she gets some much-needed rest and you get to bond with the baby. Really. Seeing that cherubic face looking at you while feeding is a joy every father should experience.

You're off the hook, though, for the first 4 weeks or so. Why? Because introducing a bottle to your baby too soon increases the chance of your baby rejecting the breast and preferring the bottle. (It's easier to extract liquid from a bottle than a breast, remember?) So be aware of this.

One thing I'd like to mention at this juncture: if your wife chooses to breast-feed but is unable due to illness or some other reason, be extra supportive. It's a delicate subject that no man will ever fully comprehend, so please be more understanding of your wife's needs during this fragile transitional period.

With that said, if you and your wife choose to bottle-feed for whatever reason, you should—and will—help out. In addition to taking over some of the feedings, including the middle-of-the-night ones, there are bottles to clean, nipples to sterilize, formula to buy, and powder to mix. And as your child gets older, you have different kinds of nipples and bottles to buy and sterilize. Your formula choice may change, too.

There's a lot of hit and miss when it comes to bottle-feeding. For instance, your baby might not take to the new nipples you recently bought. But just keep trying until you find ones that work.

Same goes for formula. There are a lot of different types and brands out there. If you strike out once, twice, maybe even three times, don't worry, you'll eventually find the one that junior will lap up with reckless abandon.

Also, please be extremely careful if you warm up formula in the microwave. The heat is not evenly distributed and can cause hot spots which can scorch your baby's mouth. Shaking it helps, and so does testing the temperature of the liquid on your skin.

Hey, you know how good it feels to let out a nice, big, deep-down-from-your-soul belch after a sumptuous meal? Your baby feels the same way, that's why you need to burp your little one after feedings. Simply place the young'un over your shoulder and pat him or her on the back until you hear *"urp."* Or set the baby on your knee, bend him slightly forward with one hand supporting the neck and chest area, and pat him on the back. (The nurses in the maternity ward taught me this technique.) But don't forget, place a burp cloth in a strategic location before you do any patting, unless you enjoy smelling like fermented yak's milk.

Which brings us to, of course, the spit-up. Sometimes it's just a small amount, other times it's like projectile vomiting. Each child is different, too. With our youngest, Alex, we were constantly getting our carpet steam-cleaned because he'd spit up with such frequency, and for months on end. I got the distinct feeling he enjoyed it, too, because he always had this satisfied smile on his face after he did it. Either that or he enjoyed watching Mommy and Daddy's spastic attempts at trying to "catch it" before the volatile liquid soiled our beige Berber carpet again.

Our oldest? Another story altogether. Zach didn't spit up much, but when he did—thar she blows! When Zach was an infant, my wife's brother, Brian, came to visit after work. He had a client meeting that day and was dressed in his best bib and tucker. I had just finished feeding Zach and was lying him down on the changing table. Brian walked in the room and I looked at Zach and said, "Look, it's Uncle Brian, do you love your Uncle Brian?" At that precise moment Zach let fly a stomach full of warm, fetid formula—I swear, 4 feet across the room, all over his uncle's new Hugo Boss suit!

His aim—and timing—could not have been any better. We roared with laughter. Needless to say, their relationship has rebounded.

Here's some consolation. Around the 4- to 6-month mark, you can start to introduce solid foods. Hurray. Again, take over some feedings. Make it fun. Play the airplane game, you know, pretend the spoon is an airplane coming in for a landing. Stuff like that.

But don't force the food down their throat. Let them lick the food from the spoon at first, then after a while they'll get the hang of it and you can place the spoon in their mouth. Rice and cereals are good to start with, then you can move to vegetables, fruits, and eventually meats.

In Chapter 52, I explain my position on introducing jarred vegetables before jarred fruit. For the full explanation, simply skip to that chapter. If you're tired because you've been up all night feeding the baby, just take my word for it—feed them vegetables before introducing sweet fruit. My theory is not scientific by any means, it's just from my experience.

When I was a new father and sleep deprivation started taking its toll, someone said the wisest thing I ever heard, and it got me through many an evening:

"The nights are long, but the years are short."

Remember that when it's 4:30 in the morning and you're holding your little one in your arms. Because, before too long, your little one won't be so little anymore.

"The baby's crying again, sweetie. I'll take this one, you go back to sleep."

"Zzzzzzzzzzz ..."

GOOD DAD

BAD DAD

DO

SAY THESE TWO THINGS TO YOUR CHILDREN EVERY DAY

1. I'm proud of you.

2. I love you.

*"I'm proud of you,
and I love you very
much. Sweet dreams
and God bless ....
Good night!"*

*"Go to bed, son,
you're blocking
the TV."*

GOOD DAD

BAD DAD

DON'T

CHOOSE ODD OR "DIFFERENT" NAMES FOR YOUR KIDS

Celebrities do it. Rock stars do it. But that doesn't mean you have to do it. No, I'm not talking about trashing hotel rooms, punching out the paparazzi, or dating Playboy models. I'm talking about giving your kids oddball names.

I don't know what some of these parents are thinking. They're not the ones going through life saddled with some half-baked moniker because mom and dad thought it'd be cute. To me, it's more of an ego thing for the parents than a true sign of love for the child.

Names are powerful. It's like your own personal "brand." A boy named Burke will be perceived differently than, say, one named Myron. And I don't care how pretty a girl is, if her name is Bertha, she's going to have problems.

Don't believe me? Then why do so many celebrities change their names? Would John Wayne be the icon he is if he stuck with his real name of Marion Morrison? And Norma Jeane Baker doesn't quite have the same sex appeal as Marilyn Monroe, does it?

FATHER FIGURE

Worldwide, 1 in 25 men are not the biological father of a child they believe is theirs (approx. 4 percent)

I admit, I may be a little touchier on this subject than some, but that's because of my name. David George. Simple enough, right? Nothing screwy or oddball about it. However, it does consist of two first names. I'm telling you, I always hated the first day of school—*hated* it—because, without fail, the teacher would think my first name was George. The class would laugh. The teacher would apologize. But the damage was done. The genie was out of the bottle and I knew, come recess, I'd hear all the taunts:

"Hey George, what's your last name?"

"George, George, George of the Jungle ..."

Or the one I despised the most, sung like the song ... *"Hey there, Georgie Girl ..."*

Look, kids are kids, and they're going to find some way to tease no matter what. So why give them fodder by giving your children names that are out of the ordinary, or downright weird? You're not the one who has to live with the goofball name, your child is, so why do it?

And while we're on the subject, use the common spelling for your child's name, not some nutso one. For example, I came across this name just the other day: Cydney. Oh, brother. So, what, do you pronounce it like the city in Australia, or the organ in your body? Give me a break. And don't fall for fad names either. Fads fade fast. Names last a lifetime.

If you insist on being creative with your child's name, here's a story that might help: an old college buddy of mine was with his wife vacationing in Florida— during Hurricane Lily. The weather was atrocious and there wasn't much to do except go to the hotel bar, knock back a few margaritas, and go up to the room, if you know what I mean. Nine months later they're blessed with a beautiful baby daughter. Her name? Lily. See? Nothing weird or flaky, but still creative.

So if you don't want your kid getting beat up at recess, just stick with the basics when it comes to choosing a name. Jim. Joe. Mike. Rick. Mary. Patty. Kathy. Debbie. Whatever. Be the Good Dad and choose a good, solid name.

"It's settled then: Christopher if it's a boy, Sara if it's a girl."

"I've got it: Xerxes!"

GOOD DAD

BAD DAD

51

DO

SET UP A
LIVING TRUST

"Trust me."

If someone says these two little words to you, run as fast as you can in the opposite direction. But as one Good Dad to another, trust me when I say this: financially speaking, this is the most important chapter in the book. In fact, your undivided attention is required as you read it.

With that in mind, if you have to go see a man about a horse, do it now. Hungry? Thirsty? Get off your butt and feed your need, because I don't want you getting distracted or losing focus. Go ahead—do what you have to do. But hurry, I don't have all day.

(3¹/₂ minutes later)

Okay, are you all set? Has your hunger been sated? Your thirst slaked? Is Mr. Happy happy? Great, then let's begin.

You need a living trust, plain and simple. No doubt about it. It's the single most important part of your estate planning.

What's that you say? You're not a rich guy, and you don't have an "estate"? Let's see … because you're reading this book, I assume you have kids, or will shortly. I'm also going to assume you have a house, a checking account, a money market account, a life insurance policy, a college fund or two, some stocks, some bonds, maybe even an IRA or 401(k). These are what you call assets. Your life savings. In other words, an estate. (See, you're richer than you think, big guy.)

You'll note that I assumed a lot about you and your financial situation, but I'm sure my assumptions were fairly accurate. However, this next statement I'm going to lay on you is not an assumption. I'm so sure of myself that I'll put *my* life savings on the line. Ready? Here goes …

You're going to die someday.

That's right, death is the one unfortunate consequence of life. And when you do "shuffle off this mortal coil" (that's Shakespeare—*Hamlet* to be exact), who do you want to get your money—your children or a bunch of lawyers and the government? I thought so. That's why every Good Dad needs to set up a living trust.

According to www.dictionary.com, a *living trust* is "a trust created for the trustor and administered by another party during the trustor's lifetime. The living trust may be formed because the trustor is either incapable of managing or unwilling to manage his or her assets."

Clear as mud. So, according to me, a living trust is a legal agreement designed to protect and manage your assets. A trust spells out, in detail, how you want your assets managed while you're alive and how they are to be handled and distributed if you are incapacitated or die. It is sometimes called a *revocable living trust*, because you can easily make changes whenever you want.

I'm no lawyer, and that's about as far as I'm willing to go with the legalese, but that should give you a general overview of what a living trust is. For a more in-depth explanation, go online. Log on to your state's Bar Association website, for example, and you'll find a briefcase full of information about what makes a living will tick, and how the whole process works.

For those Good Dads with short attention spans, here's the abridged version: basically, have the paperwork/documentation drafted by a legal professional, retitle all your assets to the trust (also called funding the trust), name your beneficiaries, then dictate how you want your assets distributed upon your death or incapacitation.

Now, do realize there is more detail and legwork involved in creating a trust than that, but the point I'm trying to convey is that setting up a trust is not complicated.

What's the easiest part of having a living trust? The part when you die. (Sorry, big fella, but we have to talk about it.) Yes, when you kick the bucket, that's when a living trust kicks into high gear. Because you've officially transferred your entire estate to the trust, and the trust has explicit instructions on how to distribute your assets and possessions when you die, your loved ones will be assured of getting their share quickly and easily. Yes, assured. Know why? No probate.

Let's say you die without a trust. Big mistake. You have no legal record or documentation of how you want your estate handled, so your estate goes into the black hole known as probate court. Complicated, messy, expensive probate court. What you own and how your assets are distributed are now under control of the court and your state's laws governing that sort of thing. And if you think these laws were written to benefit you and your family's individual situation, you are sorely mistaken. Attorney's fees, court costs, and taxes will eat up your assets faster than you can say *habeus corpus*. The only thing that's not fast is the process, which could drag on for years.

No matter how you slice it, probate is a royal pain in the assets. You don't want your wife and kids wandering aimlessly through the maze of the judicial system during their time of grief only to end up being fleeced out of their fair share of the money, do you? Of course not. That's why you need to put your trust in a trust.

How much does it cost to create one? Depends. You can go online and set one up for a couple hundred bucks. (I do believe it still needs to be reviewed by a lawyer, though.) Or you can go through an attorney who specializes in estate law and spend roughly $1,000—maybe less, maybe more, depending on how complicated and detailed your individual situation is. If I were you, I'd spend the dough and go to an attorney. Setting up a trust is extremely important, and you want to make sure it's done correctly. Again, I'm no legal expert, that's just my own humble Good Dad opinion.

What about a living trust versus a will? Fair question, but no contest. Do the trust. A will won't keep you out of probate like a trust can; you still have to deal with the judicial system and the fees and the costs and the taxes. And if you're a private person, keep in mind that all probate transactions are a matter of public record.

If you want to cover all the bases, feel free to do both. For example, let's say you've been meaning to fund the trust with some newly acquired assets but you haven't gotten around to doing it when—wham!—you get hit by a bus. First of all, always look both ways when crossing a street. Second, in an instance such as sudden death, a will can help save your negligent butt. But if it's between a will and a trust, the trust wins, hands down.

Trust me.

"Honey, I called a lawyer; we have an appointment tomorrow at 9 a.m."

"We don't need a will. Trust me."

GOOD DAD

BAD DAD

52

DON'T

DENY YOUR KIDS SWEETS OR FAST FOOD

Want to super-size your kids? Feed them sweets and fast food. If you haven't noticed—and it's kind of hard not to—Americans are fat. And not just adults, but kids, too. Obesity is rampant in our society because of our penchant for bigger, fattier, saltier portions of just about anything you can sink your eyeteeth into.

If a 2-pound burger loaded with three bacon strips, extra cheese, half a Polish sausage, a mound of grilled onions, and drowned in a pint of secret sauce isn't enough to satisfy your hunger, or little Johnny's (and I use the word "little" loosely), you can always wash it down with a monster-size 3-gallon soft drink and chase it with an inch-thick, cloyingly sweet triple-fudge brownie made with walnuts, dusted with powdered sugar, and topped with a super-scoop of French vanilla ice cream awash in chocolate sauce. Hey, it's the American way. No wonder cosmologists say the universe is expanding—their telescopes are probably fixed on our waistlines.

At this point you're probably scratching your head thinking, "What's this guy trying to say? He's talking out of both sides of his mouth."

I don't blame you for being confounded, and I apologize. On one hand the chapter title is telling you *not* to deny your kids sweets and fast food, yet I just spent 186 words ragging on sweets and fast food and telling you how terribly unhealthy they are for your children. And it's true: they are unhealthy. Junk food and a steady diet of sweets do make people fat and they do set children up for a lifetime of poor eating habits.

However, here's where I back-pedal. In my defense, I'm not retreating from my position in a wishy-washy kind of way, but in a grounded-in-reality sort of way. Indulging your kids with sweets and fast food every now and then actually is the Good Dad thing to do.

Let's tackle the subject of sweets first. When our kids first started eating jarred baby food, we introduced them to green vegetables such as peas and green beans way before we introduced them to fruit, because we didn't want their palates to get accustomed to the sweeter fruit flavors and then reject the not-so-sweet vegetable baby food. And it worked. When they got used to vegetables, and liked them, we then acquainted them with fruit. Which, of course, was like nectar from the gods after eating strained peas for weeks on end.

After they got past the jarred baby food and moved on to real food, we were still quite vigilant in our quest to keep them from eating sweets because, again, we didn't want them to develop a "sweet tooth" and have their developing bodies crave sugar. So we stockpiled every type of fruit and kid-friendly vegetable we could get our hands on. And we were proud of ourselves.

But guess what got in the way of our grand plan? Reality. Holidays such as Halloween, birthday parties and birthday cakes, friends offering them candy, friends' parents offering them candy, *grandparents* offering them candy. And when you see that first piece of sugared confection pass through their untainted lips and into their virgin bodies, you cringe.

Of course, you don't want to be the psycho parent who rips the Tootsie Roll out of your child's mouth and throws it away while wearing HAZMAT gear. So you give in, and thus begins the years-long joust with your kids over how many sweets is too much.

Looking back, I realize we may have gone too far in keeping sweets at arms length, I mean, it's only candy, and candy is a part of childhood. But one thing I will say for my wife and me; serving our kids nothing but fruit and vegetables before introducing them to sugary sweets sure helped establish a healthier dietary pattern.

To this day they'll ask for bananas or oranges or apples when they're hungry for a snack. They'll even munch on carrots and eat broccoli and artichokes and green beans for dinner—and actually *like them*. Sure, they'll ask for a piece of chocolate—they're kids—but if we say no, they don't get upset. And if we say yes, they're all excited.

Going back to chocolate for a second, recent studies have found that dark chocolate contains antioxidants and isn't quite as "bad" for you as other lighter, more sugary milk chocolates. So instead of stashing brand-name candy bars filled with nuts and caramel and all that other crap, we keep a bag of high-quality Dove dark chocolate handy. When our kids want something sweet and we know that offering them an orange ain't gonna cut it, we give them a single piece of dark chocolate. They love it, and it makes us feel better.

Alright, I have to get something off my chest, and now seems as good a time as any: I bribe my kids with chocolate. Yes, in this instance I'm the Bad Dad. Again, reality strikes. If I've had a bad day, my energy level has dipped below zero, and I need the kids to do something, I'll bribe them. It's easier than fighting with them.

Hey, nobody ever said fatherhood was black and white. So shoot me.

Now, on to fast food.

Boy, where do I begin? Do I start by calling it by its true name, "heart attack on a bun"? Nah, that's a cheap shot. Accurate, but cheap. How about, "Fast food, where the box is better than the food." Sorry, another cheap shot. I'm now going to take the high road and say this: fast food is getting healthier. Which is a good thing, 'cause it certainly can't get much worse.

Have you ever perused one of those so-called "nutritional" charts they hang in fast food restaurants? Not much nutrition going on there, but you will find a whole lot of sodium, fat, and calories. This is why my wife and I avoided fast food like the plague with our kids. As with sweets, we didn't want them to acquire a taste for it and then crave it more and more. So we held out as long as we could. Then—wham!—reality punched me right in the nose.

Again, out of convenience, or just plain acquiescence, we caved. If they really, really, *really* want it, we throw in the towel and get them fast food. It's fun for them, and fast food—the villain that it is—does taste good, in a salty, fatty sort of way. But when you do take the little nippers through the drive-thru, you've got to be the Good Dad and think outside the cardboard box.

For one thing, steer your nestlings toward the healthier items on the menu. Plain burger, no cheese or special sauce or anything like that. Fries? Go for the smallest quantity. You can even have some fun with the person at the drive-thru and say, "Small fries for my small fry, please." Or maybe not.

If your kids like salads, by all means, get them a salad. Even kid's meals, the perennial lure that fast food chains cast in the waters trolling for kiddie customers, are now offering healthier accompaniments such as applesauce and milk instead of fries and a soft drink. Great marketing ploy. They're totally pandering, but hey, the kids benefit, so what's the harm.

Okay, I just explained to you my stance on sweets and fast food in 1,219 words. Now I'm going to sum it up in three:

Everything in moderation.

And during those times when life tosses you around a bit and you need to make things easier on yourself just to get through another day, consider adding this addendum …

Everything in moderation, including moderation.

"It's been a while, so okay kids, let's go get a burger."

"It's been since lunch, so okay kids, let's go get a burger."

GOOD DAD

BAD DAD

53

BE CREATIVE WHEN IT COMES TO YOUR WORK SCHEDULE

Unless you married rich, I'm guessing you're the breadwinner of the family. And as the breadwinner, you probably spend more time at work than you'd like.

Let's figure it out: a typical work week is 40 hours. Let's say you get 2 weeks vacation per year. Because there are 52 weeks in a year, that leaves you with 50 weeks of work per year. Multiply this number by the number of hours in a work week and that leaves you with 2,000 hours of work a year.

Each year.

Multiply 2,000 hours by 18, the approximate number of years your children will live under your roof, and what you get, my friend, is a total of 36,000 hours. Translation: 36,000 hours away from your kids.

Now, I was never very good at math, but 36,000 hours sure seems like a lot. But like all you other guys out there, I fight the good fight. I hunker down and go to my job day in and day out to support my family. I'd work my fingers down to bloody nubs to put food on the table if I had to, and I'm sure you would, too.

But wouldn't it be great if you could slice off a good-sized chunk of that 36,000-hour block of time and spend it with your kids instead of your coworkers? Boy howdy, yes. Well guess what? I'm here to tell you that it can be done, and is being done, by Good Dads everywhere with a little something called an Alternative Work Schedule.

For the uninitiated, an Alternative Work Schedule, sometimes called Flexible Work Options, is an arrangement between an employee and an employer where the employee sets his own work schedule. The goal? Achieving a healthier balance between work, family, and personal responsibilities. It's a notion that's really catching fire.

But let's back up for a minute. The whole American ethic of work, work, work is so ingrained in our culture that we, as employees, don't balk at the amount of time employers expect us to work. Consequently, the mindset of *"Thank you, sir, may I have another?"* is all too commonplace. Let me ask you this: how often have you worked more than 8 hours a day? Or worked a Saturday or Sunday? Or brought work home? That's what I thought. As more and more employers are asking more and more from their employees, more and more kids are seeing less and less of their dads. See what I'm saying, more or less? Sure you do.

Enter the Alternative Work Schedule, which offers you several options, including …

- Flextime

- Telecommuting

- Job-sharing

- Compressed work week

- Part-time

Flextime is having flexibility in arrival or departure times—arrive a little later, leave a little later. Pretty simple. Telecommuting is working from home, usually 1 to 2 days a week, connected to work via computer, PDA, e-mail, and so on. Job-sharing is sharing, or splitting, the responsibilities of one full-time position between two people. A compressed work week is working more hours per day but fewer days per week, usually four 10-hour days instead of five 8-hour days. And if I have to explain what part-time is, you shouldn't have procreated in the first place, Gilligan. It's time to get out of the gene pool. Now.

As you mull over your options, keep in mind that some are easier to pull off than others. Flextime is probably the easiest. You still come to work everyday, and you still work the same number of hours. Bosses like that. Telecommuting is the second easiest. Again, you work the same amount of hours, you're just spending some of them in a different location. A compressed work week might be mutually beneficial because the number of hours is the same, but if you already work 10-hour days *five* days a week (which a lot of people are these days), this wouldn't be the smartest approach.

That leaves us with job-sharing and part-time which, in my mind, are the toughest to pull off. But if you've got a good solid case to back up your argument, hey, go for it. But definitely check to see if your paycheck, benefits, or medical insurance will be affected. If so, that could put the kibosh on your plans.

Speaking of making a good solid case, do your homework and present a bulletproof proposal to your boss, so he (or she) can't refuse your offer. And don't be a wuss about it. You don't work for Vlad the Impaler. A vital appendage will not get lopped off if you ask.

That said, you can't just barge into your boss's office with both guns blazing and tell him how terrific an Alternative Work Schedule will be for you. No, no, no, tell him how wonderful it will be for him and the company. How it will boost your productivity and make you a more valuable asset to the company. Spin it in such a way that it sounds good for you, but *great* for the company.

Is your boss environmentally conscious? Working from home 2 days a week, or going into work 4 days a week instead of 5, will cut down on your commuting time, thus cutting down on emissions, thus cleaning the air, thus making the world a better place for all God's creatures. See? Spin, baby, spin.

But remember, the point to an Alternative Work Schedule is to spend more time with your family, not more time on the golf course. Think about it. How great would it be to walk your daughter home from kindergarten one day a week, holding hands and talking about the ballerina picture she drew that day? Or to take your son to a park in the afternoon and watch him go down the big slide for the first time? Pretty freakin' great, if you ask me.

Are you a workaholic? Now that you've got a family, it's time to become a lifeaholic. Kick that Type-A personality of yours into overdrive and put your energy into your kids instead of your job.

And in your next life? Marry rich.

"On their death bed, no one ever said, 'I wish I spent more time at the office.'"

GOOD DAD

"You know, this cubicle is just like home to me."

BAD DAD

54

DON'T

BUY USED
CAR SEATS

Used cars? Sure.

Used furniture? Why not?

Used clothes? What the heck?

Used car seats? Not on your life. Or should I say, not on your child's life. Because that's who you're putting in jeopardy.

On the surface, used car seats make sense. New ones are expensive and used ones can be snatched up at a bargain. This savings can be awfully enticing, especially if you're the wheelman of a two-car family where you'll need car seats for each vehicle—double the number of car seats, double the expense.

Then, of course, as your kids get older you go from infant seats to forward-facing seats to booster seats. Cha-ching, cha-ching, cha-ching. It all adds up, so you might as well cut corners where you can, right? Wrong. What looks good on the balance sheet doesn't necessarily translate into real life. Used car seats may be less costly, but they can also be more dangerous.

For example, you're at a garage sale and you spy a car seat that looks decent and so does the price. So you snatch it up before some other frugal father does. Let me ask you this: Do you know the history of that car seat? Was it ever in an accident? Is it missing any parts? Does it come with the original instruction manual? These are things you need to know.

If it was in an accident, there could be hairline fractures or cracks that aren't noticeable to your eye but can weaken the seat to the point of failure if it's in another crash. Yes, that's right, the crash your child may be in. Why do you think you're *buying* a car seat, anyway?

If it's missing any parts, how would you know? If it doesn't come with an instruction manual, how are you going to know if it's installed properly? And what if the seat was recalled since the original purchase due to a flaw in the design? You'd never know that either.

The one instance where buying a used car seat might be okay—and this is still a mighty big *might*—is if you're buying it from a relative or close friend and you know with 100 percent certainty it was never in a crash. But even that's risky. Just through normal wear and tear, straps can become frayed, parts can become brittle, components can become weak—and you'll never know until the unthinkable happens.

Now that you know what not to do, here's what you need to do: spring for a new car seat.

There are a lot of makes and brands on the market, in all price ranges. Sure, you'll see the top of the line ones that carry a designer label and have all the bells and whistles. But do you really need the most expensive one to safeguard your child? Nah. Sometimes the expensive ones are just more complicated to use. Find the one in your price range and buy it. Yes, it will be more expensive than a used one, but well worth the peace of mind.

If you have any questions or would like more information on car seats, call the National Highway Traffic & Safety Association at 1-888-DASH-2-DOT or log on to nhtsa.gov. They'll take care of you.

Do Good Dads treat their kids like crash test dummies? No they do not, that's why Good Dads buy new car seats, not used car seats.

And that's where I stand on the subject of sitting.

"Brand new, installed, and ready to go."

"Hey, hon, look what I found on the curb! And to think they were going to throw away this perfectly good car seat. What were

GOOD DAD

BAD DAD

55

DO

MAKE TIME FOR YOUR WIFE AND YOUR MARRIAGE

Remember when "making time" with your wife meant having—how shall I phrase this—sexual congress? Sadly, several years and several children later, making time with your wife is now defined as putting forth extra effort just to spend some *time* with her.

What with the kids and the preschool and the dog and the dishes and the laundry and the cleaning and the PTA and the pediatrician and the diapers and the vacuuming and the grocery shopping and the cooking, it leaves precious little time for spending any time with your wife, let alone any time for lovemaking. In my book, this is totally unacceptable. Tell your wife that congress is back in session and your jurisdiction is all territories south of the border, if you catch my drift.

All kidding aside, spending some alone time with your wife and playing caretaker to your marriage is an extremely important part of fatherhood.

It's like that age-old riddle about which came first, the chicken or the egg? Only in this instance it's what comes first, the children or your marriage? My answer to this conundrum is that *neither* has to come first, but the two shall coexist in a perfectly seamless, symbiotic relationship. Obviously your kids need you, but so does your wife.

It's easy to let your marriage fall into disrepair when kids come along. And it's such a slow erosion process that it's barely noticeable. You just wake up one morning and realize that you don't kiss your wife goodbye anymore, you no longer hold hands, you don't make her laugh as much as you used to.

These are the small warning signs that things might be in decay, but that doesn't mean that things are over. Far from it. There are several measures you can take to prevent the situation from getting worse.

First and foremost, set aside one night a week for Date Night, usually Saturday night. (If you can't afford one night a week, because it usually involves getting a babysitter, do it once a month, but try not to go any longer than that.) Date Night is just that, you and the spousal unit go on a date. A real, honest-to-goodness, opening-the-car-door-for-your-wife kind of evening.

Spice it up, too. Buy her a box of chocolate truffles or some lingerie. Bring your A-game and do what you have to do to make it exciting and special. You won't go all out like this every Saturday night, of course, but every now and then, why the heck not? She's the mother of your children—she deserves it.

Right after the birth of our second child, I surprised my wife one night by showing up in a very pricey (rented) Jaguar XK convertible. Black. My sister arrived shortly after to babysit. I then escorted my wife to her awaiting coach and took her to a beachside restaurant overlooking the Pacific. Driving up and down the coast in that Jag droptop was a real thrill for her. (Getting the girl by getting the car, just like in high school!) But what made the night even more special was that it was the anniversary of our first date. To this day, we not only celebrate our wedding anniversary but our "dating" anniversary, too.

You don't have to do anything that extravagant to make time for your wife and your marriage, though. Small gestures can make just as big a statement. Surprise her some night with a bouquet of fresh flowers. Not just any flowers, mind you, but the kind you had at your wedding. We had champagne-colored roses at our nuptials, so when I bring home flowers, I try to find those. When I hand them to her I see that sparkle in her eyes that hooked me oh-so-many years ago. And after not seeing it for awhile, it's a welcome sight, believe me.

Another idea is to give her a massage. Not just a shoulder rub, but a full-on, full-body, deep-tissue rub with scented massage oil, soft music, candlelight, and a glass of champagne with a single strawberry in it. For that extra touch, throw some rose petals on the bed. Man oh man, talk about sexual congress. I guarantee you the subject of impeachment will never come up. But something else will.

Can you get a family member to take the kids for a night? Ooh-la-la, take them up on it. When our kids were real little my in-laws offered to take them for a 24-hour period so we could get away. It was a generous offer and we were very thankful, but we just didn't feel right leaving them with someone else when they were so young. In hindsight, it would've been fine, but we were new parents and a bit paranoid. But now when they offer, we practically throw the kids at them. "Here, take 'em!"

Our usual course of action is to make reservations at this one hotel that's near both our house and my in-law's. That way we're not too far away if something should happen. Adjacent to the hotel is our favorite restaurant, a splendid French bistro. We check in to the hotel, go to the room, and let relaxation be our guide.

After several hours of reading or just talking, we get dressed, go downstairs, and saunter into the restaurant. When our long, leisurely repast ends, we simply hop an elevator back to the room and do what comes naturally to a husband and wife. Yes, sometimes it's just catching a good night's sleep. Spending the night away like this happens once in a great while, but when it does, it's like vacationing at a spa. The irony of all this? *We talk about the kids the entire time.* So it goes.

Is your wife pregnant with your first, second, third, fourth, or tenth child? Then you'll need to be extra sensitive and extra attentive. For one thing, you've got the whole hormonal matter to deal with. The ups, the downs, the I-want-to-cut-your-heart-out-with-a-rusty-butter-knife look she gives you when you inadvertently say the wrong thing.

On top of this, you've got the extremely sensitive issue of body image to pay heed to. No matter how many times you tell her how great she looks and how sexy she is, all she sees in the mirror is a fat remnant of her former self—and it's all your fault. So be patient, be loving, and be careful what you say, because it could be used against you in a court of law.

Minding your marriage isn't necessarily what you think of when you enter fatherhood. But the Good Dad thinks about it. He thinks about his kids, his wife, and his marriage, because the strength of his marriage—and the relationship with his wife—is the glue that keeps everything, ahem, humming along.

Don't you agree, Congressman?

"Sweets for the sweet."

"Voted out of office? I don't get it."

GOOD DAD   **BAD DAD**

56

DON'T

TRY TO BE THE "PERFECT DAD"

Fatherhood is the single greatest experience you will ever encounter in life. (Unless you're Hugh Hefner.) I'm convinced of that.

Taking on the role of "dad" comes with rewards beyond human imagination. Having children will warm your heart and satisfy your soul like nothing else. And the love you feel for them … oh my God … is so deep, so strong, so infinite, it's almost scary. You think you love your wife? You think you love your parents? That's nothing compared to the way you love your children.

Conversely, fatherhood will blindside you with challenges and emotions and responsibilities that were unfathomable to you before you had kids. And you're never prepared for these challenges because you never know what problem might rear its ugly head. Or when.

Okay, shake it off, big guy. Because after this reality sinks in and you realize that your new role takes precedence over anything else, you'll want to step up to the plate and hit it out of the ballpark every single time a challenge arises. Meaning, you'll want to do everything *perfectly*. It's human nature. Molding, shaping, and guiding another human being through life (read: fatherhood) is a task where you get one chance, and one chance only. And as they say at Mission Control, "Failure is not an option."

In the long run, this is true. You cannot, and must not, fail. But let me tell you a little something while I have your ear: *along the way, you will fail*. So get used to it.

Think back to your own childhood. Things weren't always rainbows and lollipops, were they? I'm sure your dear ol' dad made his share of mistakes—unbeknownst to you of course. But you got through it relatively unharmed (except for that spasmodic facial tic, but we won't mention that).

Let's look at it through another facet of the prism. You know how comedians are always joking about parents and how these hapless moms and dads will inevitably screw up their kids somehow because of their parenting skills, or lack thereof?

Well, they're right. Sort of. At some point, you'll make the wrong call on a certain decision and your son or daughter will have to deal with the consequences. And it's going to hurt you more than a well-placed kick in the crotch.

But here's a little salve to put on that gaping wound called remorse: I recently read that a "perfect" childhood can actually be a detriment to children, because it doesn't prepare them for real life. As we all know, the real world is a highly competitive, dog-eat-dog jungle, and when these "sheltered" kids leave the nest, they get a nasty jolt of reality that's almost too much for them to handle.

So you see, by screwing things up every now and then, you're actually doing your kids a favor!

The bottom-line is, you're human, not perfect. You never were perfect, you never will be perfect—even when it comes to fatherhood. And the sooner you realize this, the better off you'll be.

Makes perfect sense, doesn't it?

"Oh well, chalk that up to experience."

"I'm a failure!!"

GOOD DAD

BAD DAD

57

DON'T

CLING TO
BAD DAD GUILT

(Scene 1: Dramatic courtroom setting)

Judge: Order in the court! Order in the court! Answer the question, Mr. Wilson.

Lawyer: I'll repeat it for the defendant, your honor. Mr. Wilson, on Saturday, April 22, did you or did you not say you would help your son, Timmy, practice catching a baseball?"

Mr. Wilson: Yes, yes I did.

Lawyer: In fact, you used the words, "I promise, Timmy," did you not, Mr. Wilson?

Mr. Wilson: Yes.

Lawyer: But you didn't help Timmy practice catch a baseball, did you, Mr. Wilson?

Mr. Wilson: But I …

Lawyer: Just answer the question, Mr. Wilson.

Mr. Wilson: No, I did not.

Lawyer: What did you do instead of helping your son, Timmy, practice catching a baseball, Mr. Wilson? (Pause) The court is waiting, Mr. Wilson. What did you do instead?

Mr. Wilson: I played golf!

(The courtroom erupts into audible gasps.)

Lawyer: No more questions, your honor.

Mr. Wilson: Timmy, I'm sorry! Daddy loves you!

Jury Foreman: We, the jury, find the defendant, Mr. Thomas Wilson, guilty of being the Bad Dad.

Mr. Wilson: I'm sorry, Son, will you ever forgive me?

Timmy: Yeah, Dad, no big deal. But will you forgive yourself?

Ah, the key question: will you forgive yourself?

In the previous chapter I wrote about the Perfect Dad and how there is no such animal; how we're all human and we all make mistakes, even when it comes to fatherhood. But as the exaggerated courtroom scenario points out, somewhere along the line you're going to make some Bad Dad blunder where you say, "What was I thinking?"

Oh, well. You can't unring a bell. But what you can do is let go of the guilt and move on. Don't let it eat you up inside. Some dads beat themselves up for days, months, even years, over some of the decisions they've made. Try not to let this happen to you. Just take it all in stride and chalk it up to the School of Hard Knocks. And don't overcompensate for your mistakes, either. Buying your kids some extravagant gift could make them expect some flashy toy every time things don't go as planned.

Here's what I want you to do: look back at all the sacrifices you've made for your children. All the time you've spent with them. All the good experiences you've had. Okay, do you have a crystal clear mental image of everything? Good. Because I'm sure you'll see that the Good Dad things you've done for your kids *far* outweigh any Bad Dad mistakes.

In the end, don't be so hard on yourself. Let go of the Bad Dad guilt. And you never know, maybe you'll get time off for good behavior.

"I'm sorry, Sierra, I'll make it up to you, I promise."

"I'm sorry, Sierra, I'll make it up to you, I promise. Howza 'bout a pony?"

GOOD DAD

BAD DAD

58

DO

KEEP YOUR EYE OUT FOR BAD INFLUENCES

"This is your child's brain.

This is your child's brain under the influence of bad kids.

Any questions?"

Sad but true. Not only do you have to worry about your kids being under the influence of drugs, but also under the influence of other kids. Bad kids. And they're just as harmful.

It's inevitable. Somewhere, somehow, your son or daughter will run across another kid, a so-called friend, who will influence them to take risks they normally wouldn't take, or pollute their minds with noxious ideas. Because you can't be with your kids 24/7, it's extremely difficult to keep your kids from being "under the influence."

However, there are a few things you can do that might help when faced with this all-too-common problem. First, figure out exactly why you feel a certain child is a bad influence. Size him or her up and determine if the child's influence is simply annoying, moderately disturbing, or downright dangerous.

For example, are the kid's clothes, hairstyle, or manner of speech offensive to you in some way? Maybe it's just a misunderstanding on your part. One way to handle this is to take a wait-and-see approach. Let the friendship play out. Or perhaps even die out.

Another approach is to ask your son or daughter why they like this particular child. Getting them to articulate the qualities he or she finds appealing might be difficult, but if you do succeed, it could be a real eye opener.

Or better yet, get to know the child yourself. Invite him or her over for dinner, or take everybody to a sporting event—anywhere you can talk. Observe and size up the relationship firsthand.

And don't be afraid to ask questions, either. How's your family? How many brothers and sisters do you have? What are your interests? Do you have any goals? What do you want to be when you grow up? Getting to know the child's background and personality could change your perception. Or confirm your worst fears.

If the latter is true, steer your child away from the toxic relationship ASAP. Direct them toward other kids, or engage them in other interests. If you take this approach, be honest with your son or daughter. Explain to them why you're handling the situation this way and why you think so-and-so is a bad influence. They just might see the light and agree with you.

Of course, if you *must* ban all contact, then by all means, do it. And let your child know in no uncertain terms that there will be serious consequences if they break the ban. Sure, you risk becoming extremely unpopular in the eyes of your child, but stand tough. You're the dad, they're the child. One caveat: this approach could backfire, making the bad influence even more alluring. So be careful.

As the Good Dad, you put in a lot of blood, sweat, and tears to teach your children right from wrong and to behave properly. Then all of a sudden—wham!—out of the blue comes some kid who undoes all your hard work. It's extremely frustrating and can create a lot of anger and resentment. Unless you take the appropriate measures.

Remember, bad influences happen to good kids. But Good Dads happen to good kids, too.

"I have an extra ticket for the game tonight. You want to invite Jesse? I'd like to get to know him a little better."

GOOD DAD

"Sure, you can sleep over at Jesse's, but who's Jesse?"

BAD DAD

59

DON'T

TAKE ANY TYPE OF BULLYING LIGHTLY

Did you know that approximately 75 percent of all kids fall victim to some form of bullying before they reach high school? 75 percent. That's 3 out of 4 kids! (See how quickly I did the math? Not bad for a liberal arts major.)

Help me out here, but don't schools these days have a zero tolerance policy when it comes to guns, drugs, and violence? And isn't bullying a type of violence? An emotional and psychological violence that leaves scars, albeit invisible ones? If so, then why is bullying so rampant, maybe even blindly tolerated, in our schools?

In my day, if you were picked on or teased, you simply toughed it out. You defended yourself the best way you could without getting your butt kicked, or you slinked away with your tail between your legs hoping the girl you had a crush on didn't see you quaking in abject terror. Being bullied was treated merely as a coming-of-age ritual, akin to getting a wedgie.

But people are smarter these days. They now have evidence that bullying, no matter what form it takes—physical, social, or verbal—is extremely damaging to the child being victimized. One recent study found that kids who fall prey to these playground pit bulls have more behavioral problems than kids who don't, such as being withdrawn or depressed, feeling anxious, or being genuinely unhappy at school (which doesn't make for the best learning environment). It doesn't stop at childhood either. Researchers have also found that kids who were bullied in childhood suffer more mental health problems as adults.

For all these reasons and more, you can't, as the Good Dad, tolerate bullying in any way or form. If you suspect your child is being bullied, nip it in the bud. Find out who the aggressor is and go to a person who has authority over the little cretin. A teacher, a coach, whoever. And get it stopped.

Got girls? Bullying doesn't begin and end with carriers of the Y chromosome. Girls are just as big of bullies as boys are, they just do it in stealthier ways. Instead of pushing or hitting or spitting they resort to more covert means such as social exclusion, name-calling, or intimidation.

What type of child is usually the one to get bullied? Unfortunately it's the boy or girl who is more timid, cautious, or insecure—you know, the type who probably won't fight back. The bully knows this, and that's why he or she will choose this type of child to victimize.

Like I said earlier, if your child is being bullied, tell someone of authority and have them put a stop to it. Pronto. But as the Good Dad, there are other ways to help, too. First, bolster your child's self-confidence by encouraging him or her to participate in a sport or activity they're interested in or good at.

Second, help your child establish a strong social network of friends. Remember, there's strength in numbers.

And third, teach him or her to fight back. By that I don't mean fisticuffs or derringers at 20 paces. What I do mean is arm them with an unexpected phrase or comment to say to the bully to catch the thug off guard. A surprise verbal attack, if you will. If you're a quick wit, teach your child some snappy one-liner or flip comeback to help defuse the situation.

On the flip side, (no, not that flip, the other flip), what do you do if your child is the bully? I hate to say this, but you'll probably have to take a good, hard look at your child's home life. Is there a lot of anger in the house? Is there more negative reinforcement than positive? How do *you* handle anger? Do older siblings bully the smaller ones?

I'm not a psychologist, I'm just a dad, but in my research on this subject I found that these are some of the things that can lead to bullying behavior in children. And remember, I said *can*. Some kids are just naturally aggressive or dominating or intimidating. They're people, and some people just can't help being themselves. Which is no excuse, mind you, so you still need to look at things in a rational manner and take action to rectify what could be the problem.

Long gone are the days of benign bullying. These schoolyard hooligans need to be stopped. And if you can help out in any way, bully for you.

"Next time it happens, here's what you say ..."

"I remember giving my first wedgie ... that kid's underwear was so far up his butt crack that ..."

GOOD DAD

BAD DAD

60

DO

UNDERSTAND YOUR CHILDCARE OPTIONS

Remember back when you and your wife were considered DINKS? You know, Double Income No Kids? Man, those were the days. I don't know about you, but my wife and I were as free spending as a couple of drunken swabbies on shore leave.

Of course, when the kids came along, everything changed. We went from Double Income No Kids to Double Income With Kids, then eventually *One* Income With Kids. (Sniff, sniff ... tears are welling up in my eyes as I write this ... I miss my disposable income so much!)

Whether your wife is a working mom and still bringing home a paycheck (you lucky dog, you) or if she's decided to be a stay-at-home mom (which means she works even *harder* than she did behind a desk), at some point you'll probably consider some form of childcare.

As with anything else, there are pros and cons to the various types of childcare. Some people eschew outside care altogether. Hey, to each his own. However, if you and the Mrs. do decide on childcare, the following list will give you a general idea of what to expect:

PRESCHOOL/DAYCARE CENTERS:

When one thinks of childcare, this category is usually top-of-mind. Why? Because these centers and facilities are everywhere. There's a wide variety to choose from, too. Some take infants, others don't. Some require that children be potty-trained, others don't. Whichever one you choose, make sure it works for your particular situation.

And do your homework—visit the center you're interested in, talk to the director, even sit in on the room. Get to know the school and see how it works. Oh yeah, and make sure they have an open-door policy, so you can drop in anytime.

The upside of these facilities, in addition to the preceding comments, is that the teachers usually have some form of child-development training (which is key), the environment is similar to what your kids will encounter at school, and they help children socialize with their peers. It doesn't hurt either that child-development specialists endorse a high-quality preschool as being beneficial to young children.

The downside? They can be pricey. (Kiss those Benjamins goodbye.) In addition, kids have a tendency to get sick more often because of the contact they have with other children. However, recent studies show that in the long run this may actually be better because they'll get sick less often after they start "real" school.

All in all, preschool and daycare centers are an all-around good bet.

NANNY/IN-HOUSE CARE:

This is the option I tried to sell my wife on, but she put her size-6 foot down and told me in no uncertain terms that she wanted nothing to do with it. Of course, my begging and pleading for a college-aged Swedish *au pair*—preferably twins—may have been a contributing factor to her decision, I'm not sure. But Swedish *au pairs* aside, a nanny is another viable option.

What's convenient about this setup is that a nanny will come right to your house. How cool is that? And the kids get to remain in the comfort of their own home, making them nice and secure. Another plus is that the nanny cares for your children and your children only, not a whole classroom, so your kids get the individual attention they need. Some nannies even do the cooking and cleaning. (Your wife will salivate over that one.)

Okay, now for a few minuses. With a nanny, your children won't socialize with other kids as much, and socialization is an important aspect of childhood. And then there's the cost. Nannies can be very expensive. But if both you and your wife are working, money may not be an issue.

What could be an issue, however, is this: your nanny will be alone with your children. All alone. With no one else around. So they can do whatever they want without the risk of getting caught. See what I'm driving at? Sure you do, I can see the little lightbulb over your head right now.

You've watched those news programs where a reporter will put a "nanny-cam" inside a teddy bear and film the nanny abusing a child. It's a horrible scenario to watch. Can you imagine it being your own child?

To help avoid a situation such as this, it would behoove you to check out several services, not just one. And make sure they're reputable ones. After you do a bit of legwork, choose the one you feel most comfortable with and start interviewing candidates.

Ask questions. And ask for references. Call the references and ask *them* questions. Be thorough. Then, when you feel comfortable with your choice, introduce the nanny to your kids and see if they feel comfortable with her, too. If they don't, keep searching. Leave no stone unturned.

You're not going to find the next Mary Poppins, but, as I've said before, you can never be too safe when it comes to your children.

DAYCARE PROVIDER AT THEIR HOME

I know some parents who've been extremely happy with this option, but if you do go with this arrangement please proceed with caution. For one thing, these providers vary greatly in terms of how many children they watch per day. Are they always on the hunt for more kids? To them, more kids means more money. But to you, that dilutes the attention your children will receive.

The ages of the children can vary greatly, too. Is your child the only toddler with a group of infants? Make sure you know, because if so, your child will not have the advantage of being around other kids his or her own age.

Also, be sure the environment is up to your standards. Because it's their own home, these providers may not have as many resources as a daycare center or pre-school. More importantly, they may not have the formal child development training the teachers at a daycare facility will have.

On the upside, though, is cost. They're usually less expensive. And if you know the provider—if she's a friend or you know parents who've been happy with her services—all the better.

So there you have it. Not an exhaustive treatise on childcare, but a few thoughts to get you on your way. Do your own research, and I'm sure you'll find exactly what you and your spouse are looking for.

And if you can convince your wife to get a college-aged Swedish *au pair*, you're my new hero.

"Let's make a list of pros and cons— that should help us with our decision."

"Can't they just watch themselves?"

GOOD DAD   **BAD DAD**

61

DO

ENCOURAGE
DAILY EXERCISE

When I was a kid, my mom would say, "Go outside and play." So I would.

All day long.

From morning 'til night I was running around with my friends—unsupervised, mind you—throwing rocks, playing army, riding bikes, looking at clouds, building forts. You name it, we did it. My friends and I were in constant motion, never stopping. I'd come home for dinner, eat, and collapse. Physically exhausted. And it felt great.

It's a different world nowadays. You can't let your kids run loose anymore without an adult present. Too many freaks out there. But one thing hasn't changed. The need for kids to exercise.

According to experts, every child should strive to get 30 to 60 minutes of exercise a day, ideally 60. If you want your children to get more than that, more power to ya. Give your kids as much physical exertion as they can handle. (But don't push 'em too hard. No need to be a drill sergeant about it.)

To achieve the allotted amount of time of exercise—and to keep your kids safe at the same time—organized sports is the obvious choice. And a good one.

Pick a sport, any sport. Soccer, baseball, swimming, gymnastics, track and field, football, basketball, dancing, cheerleading, tennis, golf, martial arts (Tae Kwon Do seems to be very popular these days), or any other activity you can think of. Expose your kids to a lot of sports and see which ones stick. Not only will they become more fit, but the social and physical skills they acquire can also increase their self-esteem. And hey, who couldn't use a little ego boost every now and then?

If your kids are too young to play in an organized sport, let them ride tricycles, play tag, romp around a park, or simply have them take a walk around the block with you.

Now let's talk about you. Are you what one would consider a "slug"? Better change your sloth-like habits before your kids pick up on them. Actions speak louder than words, so be active. Show the little tykes that exercise is a part of your routine and they'll see it as a normal daily activity.

You can also try to incorporate exercise into your family vacations. For example, every winter my wife and I go skiing and bring the kids with us. We put them in ski school for half-a-day, then ski with them the other half. In the summer we go places with pools or beaches so we can swim or snorkel. And when Mommy and Daddy get tired, we supervise the kids from poolside. They get to splash around, we get to lie around. It's a beautiful thing. ("*Mesero, una mas cerveza, por favor.*")

With childhood obesity at an all-time high and Type 2 diabetes on the rise, exercise is an excellent way to help combat these two health threats.

So as the Good Dad, exercise your right—to exercise. And make sure you bring the kids along for the ride.

"C'mon, let's go outside and play some catch."

"C'mon, let's go inside and watch some TV."

GOOD DAD

BAD DAD

62

TAKE A VIDEO
INVENTORY OF
EVERY ITEM IN
YOUR HOUSE

Quick, what'd you have for dinner last Tuesday? Don't remember, do you? No worries, most people can't even remember what they had for breakfast.

Which is the precise reason you need to take a video inventory of everything in your home. From your 52-inch plasma screen TV and red-leather Barcalounger to your favorite BBQ tongs. It's the best way to remember every item you purchased over the years.

Why do you need this, you might ask? Read on for the answer, my memory challenged friend.

Let's say your house is located right smack dab in the middle of Tornado Alley. Or perched precariously on a ridge near the San Andreas Fault. Or on the bank of a flood-prone river. Or in the eye of a hurricane zone. Or on a beautiful hilltop surrounded by vast stretches of untamed chaparral during the worst drought in decades.

Catch my drift? You never know when Mother Nature might give you a good ol' spanking for living in the right place at the wrong time.

Can you say "total loss"?

Although it's true that more people live in so-called "safe" areas out of harm's way, no house is truly safe. Gas lines can leak, electrical appliances can short out, fires can start. End of sermon.

If catastrophe strikes, first, thank your lucky stars you got your family and pets out alive. Second, thank those perfectly aligned stars again that you made a video of everything you lost. Because now you have indisputable proof of, well, everything you lost, which will help you *tremendously* when you go knocking on your insurance agent's door asking to replace this, that, and the other thing.

Okay, now that you've made the decision to record your belongings, don't just go for the obvious items such as furniture and electronic gadgetry. Go through every drawer, cupboard, and closet and take inventory of all the contents. And I do mean *all*. Dishware, jewelry, crystal, clothes, CDs, DVDs, books, tools, sporting equipment, whatever you've got, get it on tape. And don't forget the outside of the house, either. For some strange reason, a lot of people seem to forget the structure itself.

Yes, taking a video of your belongings is a monumental task. And a monumental pain in the butt. Which explains why the majority of homeowners don't do it. But how else are you going to recover the total cost of your losses? Without a video, you risk putting a huge financial burden on your family which could affect your kids for years to come. And you don't want to jeopardize your kids' future and/ or education in any way, do you?

Oh, and Einstein, you may want to keep this video of yours in a place other than your house. If your video's in the rec-room closet when your humble abode is washed away during the next 100-year flood, the video—like everything else—will be on its way to French Polynesia before you can say *Huahine*.

What do you do if you don't have a video camera? Get one! You've got kids, for Pete's sake. All Good Dads should have a camcorder to record baby's first steps, recitals, Halloween, etc.

There's a saying that goes something like this: "The dullest pencil is better than the sharpest mind."

In other words, even if you take daily handfuls of gingko biloba, and feel that your mind is a steel trap, (in reality it's more like a steel sieve), you'll never, ever be able to remember everything you own. And you'll never, ever be able to prove it, either.

So do what Good Dads do. Take a video inventory.

Because you never know.

"Whew, what a task, but well worth it."

"Whew, just thinking about it gives me a headache. Think I'll watch the game on my new 52-inch plasma screen instead."

GOOD DAD   **BAD DAD**

63

DO

CELEBRATE THE INDIVIDUALITY OF YOUR CHILDREN AND OTHERS

In *Good Dad/Bad Dad: The Do's and Don'ts from the Trenches*, you learned how to create a Family Disaster Plan, perform infant CPR, and maintain a healthy sex life without Viagra. (Hey tiger, if you missed it, go back and reread Chapter 3.)

But one of the most profound pieces of information I want you to take away from this book is the statement at the top of this page. Let your eyes wander up there and read it again. Now repeat it until it's seared into your cerebral cortex. Because no matter how your children turn out, no matter what their lot in life is, remember this: they are individuals, they are one-of-a-kind, and they are to be celebrated for who and what they are.

What's just as important? Teaching your kids that this dictum of "live and let live" pertains to others as well.

If somebody speaks differently, looks differently, dresses differently, acts differently, or thinks differently, so what? Being different doesn't mean being wrong. Differences like individuality are to be celebrated, creating an ethos of equality, fairness, and tolerance.

The buzzword here? Inclusion.

If you made a list of all the people in history who truly revolutionized the world or contributed true greatness or genius to mankind, it would read like a Who's Who of nut jobs.

Look at Mozart, for example. He was a lunatic, but, oh, the music that flowed through him brings enjoyment to people of all ages to this very day. In the immortal words of Falco, "Rock me, Amadeus."

And let's not forget Albert Einstein. You could categorize him as a bit of an oddball, too, with his wildly mismatched socks and his Don King-on-acid, comb-a-phobic hair. But he didn't care. He was too busy coming up with mind-blowing notions such as the theory of relativity. Was he a little zany? Yeah. If he were alive today, would I take him out for a beer and toast his zaniness? You bet.

While we're on the subject of quirkiness, here's a story about my youngest son, Alex, when he was 5 years old and in Pony Baseball. It was the last game of the season and Alex was definitely ready for it to come to an end. He'd lost all interest in baseball and just didn't have the patience for an entire game. But we encouraged him to stick it out and told him we'd all be in the bleachers rooting for him.

Halfway through the game, with Alex's team in the outfield, I got distracted for some reason and took my eyes off the field when I heard my wife say, almost under her breath, "Oh my God, Alex is meditating." Her words confused me—they made no sense—but when I looked up, she was right.

There he was, right on the baseline between first and second, sitting in the Lotus position with his glove off, hat off, eyes closed, chin slightly raised, elbows resting on knees, and his forearms raised in the air with his thumbs and index fingers joined together forming small circles—meditating! He looked like a miniature baseball Buddha!

I could hear other parents tittering because it looked so … uncommon. I mean, when was the last time you saw a 5-year-old meditating in the middle of a baseball game? Number one, my wife and I don't meditate, so I have no idea where he got it from. And number two, why was he doing it now?

I'll admit I was a little angry at first, thinking, "Alex, what the hell are you doing?" But I couldn't help but laugh because it was so comical. He stayed like that for close to 3 minutes. Other kids were running around him on their way to second base and Alex simply stayed put, Zen-like.

After the game I certainly wasn't throwing confetti at him celebrating his unique behavior, but I couldn't be mad either. I asked him why he meditated out there and he couldn't answer me. He said he didn't know why he did it, he just did it.

I did find out, though, through his older brother Zach, that Alex had seen the wise, witch-doctor baboon from *The Lion King*, Rafiki, meditating, and had emulated him several times before—so that solved that mystery. But why he chose to do it in the middle of his last baseball game, I'll never know.

My point is that everybody marches to the beat of a different drum. Some people's drums are a bit "louder" than others, but don't worry. For every Tab A, there's a Slot B.

The world is not a kind place and things don't always go according to plan. No matter how often we teach our kids the core values of inclusion, equality, and tolerance, they're bound to notice that prejudice is everywhere and people seem to celebrate conformity over individuality. But until we master the ability to move between parallel universes—where are you when we need you, Herr Einstein?—this world is the only one we've got.

So accept your kids as they are, and teach them to accept others. Give them confidence, give them love, then give them to the world. See what happens. If you did the best you could, being the best Good Dad you could be, that's all you can ask for. You can then say to yourself, "I did my best." And be proud.

There's a place in this world for everybody. Especially good kids with Good Dads.

"Live and let live."

"Hey, I'm very open-minded. I firmly believe that everybody—and I do mean everybody— is entitled to my opinion."

GOOD DAD

BAD DAD